DEVELOPING SOCIAL
IN YOUNG CHILDREN

Howell

Howell

Developing Social Competency in Young Children

Christine A. Schmidt

Redleaf Press®
www.redleafpress.org
800-423-8309

Published by Redleaf Press
10 Yorkton Court
St. Paul, MN 55117
www.redleafpress.org

First edition 2019
Senior editor: Heidi Hogg
Managing editor: Douglas Schmitz
Cover design: Jim Handrigan
Cover photograph: iStock.com/ArtMarie
Interior design: Wendy Holdman
Typeset in Sirba
Printed in the United States of America
26 25 24 23 22 21 20 19   1 2 3 4 5 6 7 8

Library of Congress Cataloging-in-Publication Data
Names: Schmidt, Christine A., author.
Title: Developing social competency in young children / by Christine A. Schmidt.
Description: First edition. | St. Paul, MN : Redleaf Press, [2019] | Includes bibliographical
    references.
Identifiers: LCCN 2018051918 (print) | LCCN 2018054245 (ebook) |
    ISBN 9781605546544 (e-book) | ISBN 9781605546537 (pbk. : alk. paper)
Subjects: LCSH: Social skills in children. | Social skills--Study and teaching.
Classification: LCC BF723.S62 (ebook) | LCC BF723.S62 S345 2019 (print) |
    DDC 155.4/182--dc23
LC record available at https://urldefense.proofpoint.com/v2/url?u=https-3A__lccn.loc.gov
    _2018051918&d=DwIFAg&c=euGZstcaTDllvimEN8b7jXrwqOf-v5A_CdpgnVfiiMM&r=
    gX7U_27BtUCeFTyI7PMJ4yl8ifrCjuxqZQNBnwQelXg&m=PLhDzXkKiqaQQZYydd
    ybel7z1FDTXNptPkw_T5ASIHU&s=_3PH4-FwITddoCRzL3Ua9LCzxgbP1yV2tHW7cU
    _ggr4&e=

Printed on acid-free paper

To my grandchildren: Jessica, Howie, A. J., Nate, Emma, Sydney, Bella, Sophia, Chloe, S. J., Addy, Melanie, and Sam. Your zest for life, willingness to reach out to others, and ability to find the good in everyone inspired this book. Thank you for your unconditional love and for allowing me to share in your lives.

Contents

Acknowledgments

I would like to thank the many child care providers from both centers and family child care programs who participated in focus groups, conversations, and site visits with me. This book would not be a reality without your candid answers to my questions and your sharing of stories and strategies. Your dedication to the field and your willingness to create great places for children to grow and become socially competent individuals are a testament to your professionalism.

To Katie and Beth, thank you for helping when asked and for your candid conversations and willingness to ask the hard questions. To Mandy, thank you for your ability to find what I needed when I needed it.

To my family, thank you for your support and understanding while I took time away to write this book. To my husband, who has weathered the storm of this writer's life over the past year, thank you for always believing in me, supporting me, and not complaining. I will be forever grateful to you for fixing the potholes of my life.

To the staff of Redleaf Press, thank you for the opportunity to write this book. A special thanks to my editor, Christine Zuchora-Walske, for her patience and support through the editing process.

Introduction

What are social skills, and why are they so important? That's a fair question. One might think that as children grow and mature, they will naturally learn how to interact with other people. The reality is, however, that social skills are not a birthright. Children do not automatically develop these skills. In fact, children often face situations they cannot navigate appropriately because they do not have the necessary skills, language, or previous experience.

Social skills are the tools we use to communicate to others how we feel and what we need or want. According to the National Association of School Psychologists (NASP), "Good social skills are critical to successful functioning in life" (2002). Children who have strong social skills are less likely to engage in negative behaviors or experience challenging outcomes, such as substance abuse, bullying, teenage pregnancy, depression, and delinquency. They typically perform better in school, get their needs met in socially acceptable ways, and successfully navigate the many groups and social situations that each day brings.

Think of a time when you were caring for a child who seemed unreasonable, stubborn, or inconsolable. You may have thought, "Wow, this child is having a bad day." That's a natural reaction, but a more constructive response might have been to ask yourself, "What is really happening here?" or "Why does this child always seem to have problems interacting with peers?" Asking yourself what the reason for the behavior could be is a great way to determine what social skill a child might be missing—and, in turn, what you can do to teach the child that skill.

Teachers, caregivers, and parents of young children often wonder why individual children act in certain ways in social situations. Even children from the same family unit may act differently when facing the same situation. These differences are partly due to the fact that each child is born with a specific temperament. For example, some children are fearful and reluctant to try anything new, while others are feisty and go headlong into anything, believing they will do well. Still others are flexible, accommodating, and not easily angered. Temperament plays an important role in whether a child achieves or struggles to achieve social competency. Some children's temperaments make it harder for them to navigate certain social situations. For this reason, learning social skills is a lifelong process.

Children learn what to do in various life situations by watching and learning from the people around them. During any given day, a child enters and exits many group situations. The social challenges that children face can change depending on the situation or environment. Within each environment are a variety of individuals and a variety of problem-solving options—and not all options are appropriate, even if they reward children with the desired results. Children interact with many people who may or may not have positive social skills. Often children lack the knowledge and experience to be socially competent in all situations. Even adults sometimes struggle with social skills. So when children watch others, they learn both appropriate and inappropriate ways of getting their needs met.

Because social skills do not just automatically develop, because children are prewired with unique temperaments, and because other people don't always model good social skills, adults need to teach young children these skills directly. Who better to teach them than those who care for them? Adults who play major roles in the lives of children are in the best position to understand which skills children have and which they lack. Determining what social skills children need to learn, designing an environment that encourages development of these skills, and intentionally providing opportunities and activities to test and hone these skills form the foundation on which social skills can be built.

HOW THIS BOOK CAN HELP YOU FOSTER SOCIAL COMPETENCY

There are many ways to define the term *social competency*. This book defines social competency as a group of seven skill sets that enable children to interact with other people successfully so they can navigate the world around them. The skill sets, as described by educator and social psychologist Jim Ollhoff and educator Laurie Ollhoff (2007), are communication, coping, community building, conflict resolution, confidence, curiosity, and control. Each chapter will discuss a specific skill set and its associated skills. The book will define

Introduction

each skill, explain why it is important to the ongoing development of social competency, and describe how the skills in a set work together.

Within each chapter, readers will find intentional teaching strategies along with skill-building activities, environmental design ideas, and suggestions for staff and parent education. By using intentional teaching strategies and developing targeted activities, adults can model appropriate social skills and provide opportunities to help children learn these skills. Through practice and integrated activities, children will have opportunities and designated time to hone and potentially master these skills. The environment plays an essential role in helping children develop their social skills. It consists of three dimensions: temporal, interpersonal, and physical. (For more information about these dimensions, see pages 8–9 in chapter 1.) Each chapter examines the role of the adult in intentionally designing each environment and using purposeful teaching strategies within the environment to maximize a child's success. This examination is followed by staff and parent education tips providing strategies for use in everyday life. These strategies can be shared in parent and staff communication venues and can serve as topics for staff meetings or trainings. Finally, each chapter offers a list of children's books about the chapter's skill set to use in the classroom or at home. Books can introduce a specific skill, provide stories to help children discuss their feelings and understand others' feelings, or problem solve how children would handle a difficult situation. This list is just a sampling; a local librarian can assist in finding books appropriate for a child's age, cognitive ability, and reading level.

While this book discusses the social competency skill sets individually, understanding that the skill sets seldom work in isolation is important. While one skill may be listed under a specific skill set, that same skill may also be needed in another skill set. The seven skill sets and their associated skills are interwoven. They work together to form a system that enables children to navigate the world around them and the social encounters of daily life.

The information in this book comes not only from my formal education in child development and school-age care but also from my thirty-five-plus years conducting observations, offering technical assistance to programs, and mentoring staff as a national accreditation manager, state specialist, trainer, and consultant to various education programs and organizations. This experience, coupled with many years of teaching both children and the adults who teach children, has helped me gather a wealth of knowledge about the social issues children face in their day-to-day lives and how adults respond to these issues. In addition, I conducted several focus groups with caregivers, teachers, and parents of children in early care and education programs (both center-based and family child care), as well as primary school. These focus groups helped me understand and explain the challenges children face when they lack social skills. Members of the focus groups shared real-life stories that illustrate these challenges, and these stories appear in every chapter. These stories offer a window into the lives of children three to eight years old who are struggling to get their needs met appropriately. The vignettes show how a lack of social skills can manifest in everyday situations and activities.

Each child-serving program is unique in character, structure, and services offered. The children within each program come from diverse ethnic and socioeconomic backgrounds. Lack of social skills is an issue that's not limited to a specific geographical area, age, ethnicity, or culture. Being in tune with the children in your care can help you determine when children lack certain social skills. Remain proactive by creating activities and environments that support children as they learn and hone social skills, which are gifts they will use throughout their lifetime.

Understanding Social Competency

WHAT IS SOCIAL COMPETENCY?

The Encyclopedia of Children's Health (accessed 2017) states that "social competence is the condition of possessing the social, emotional, and intellectual skills and behaviors needed to succeed as a member of society." Social skills are managed by the prefrontal cortex of the brain. The prefrontal cortex continues to develop until age twenty-five. Since the prefrontal cortex is still developing well into adulthood, it is easy to see why the process of developing and refining social skills is an ongoing one. These skills do not just appear; they take time to learn and master.

Children acquire social skills through interactions with individuals they encounter in a variety of environments. Children traverse many environments and interact with many people on any given day. A child's ordinary routine may include being at home, child care, school, afternoon or evening activities, church, grandparents' home, and more. Each environment provides the child opportunities to learn from other people.

Children are aware of all that happens around them, even if they seem engaged in other activities. Children watch adults and other children to see how they handle specific situations and what skills they use to get what they want. They watch how adults deal with conflicts between children as well as conflicts between adults. Children notice what occurred and how the adults reacted to the situation. They observe what strategies the children or adults used and how successful they were in getting what they wanted. While children are viewing such situations, they may not say anything to the adults in the room; rather, children store this information until they encounter a similar situation and want a similar outcome. Children remember the situation, the strategies used, and which strategies adults thought were acceptable and unacceptable.

Reacting quickly and negatively when a social conflict or other problem occurs with children can be tempting—especially when we have discussed the situation in question many times and we believe the children should know by now what the rules are. But children forget rules easily and need frequent reminders. What is more, we must be consistent with our responses to similar situations. If we are inconsistent, we send children mixed messages. Be aware of the message you send to children when you are dealing with other people. During every interpersonal interaction, we send messages about how we think other people should be treated, about what we consider appropriate behavior, and about what we think are acceptable communication styles. If children witness people being treated differently in similar situations, they become frustrated and confused. The following vignette offers an example of this confusion.

A preschool located in an elementary school was given specific times to use the school gym for an indoor large-motor play space. The teachers instructed the children to walk at all times indoors (except when playing in the gym) because the floors were routinely waxed and could be very slippery. Steven loved to run and ran all the time. This was an ongoing problem for the staff.

The preschoolers were entering the gym to watch the end of a basketball game before they took over the gym. Steven ran into the gym and almost ran into another child who was walking to the bleachers. The staff reminded Steven to walk in order to be safe and explained that if he chose to run again before playtime, he would need to take some time to remember the rule about walking in the building. A few minutes later, Steven ran up the bleacher steps, pushing and shoving on his way.

His teacher said, "Steven, remember a few minutes ago when we talked about walking in the building? We said if you choose to run again, you would need to take a few minutes to think about the rule for walking in the building. Please sit here and take a few minutes to think about this, then come to me when you are ready to talk."

Chapter 1

In a few minutes, Steven walked up to the teacher and said he had thought about it and was ready to talk. The teacher asked, "Steven, what's the rule about running inside the building?"

He said, "We need to walk unless we are playing a game in the gym."

The teacher then asked, "Why do you think we have that rule?"

Steven said, "To keep me and my friends safe."

The teacher said, "I think you've got it now, Steven. Let's sit here until it's our turn for the gym."

About five minutes later, a preschooler named Sara came running into the gym. She ran straight to the teacher. The teacher said, "Hi, Sara, I am glad you were able to join us this morning."

Sara said, "I am so excited! The doctor says I can play outside now, and I do not have to wear my brace anymore."

The teacher said, "That is great news! We will be going outside this afternoon. Now we are waiting for our turn in the gym. This basketball game will be over in a few minutes."

Steven came up to the teacher and asked, "Why doesn't Sara have to think about the walking rule, like I did? She ran too!"

This caught the teacher off guard. She was quiet for a moment and then said, "You know, you are right. I should have talked to Sara about the walking rule." The teacher turned to Sara and reminded her of the walking rule, saying, "Sara, I know you were excited about being able to go outside, but when we are inside, we need to walk. I am worried that if you run inside, you might slip on the floor and get hurt."

Sara said, "OK, I'll remember."

The teacher later explained that Sara always followed the rules and that this infraction was out of the ordinary for her. The teacher thought that Sara ran indoors because she was so excited about her good news. Admitting to Steven that he was right and that the teacher should have talked to Sara helped Steven see that even adults make mistakes. In addition, the teacher talking to Sara using the same words she used with Steven helped him see equality in the adult response to the same situation. The teacher's good relationship with

Steven allowed him to feel comfortable enough to call her out on the inequality of the teacher's reactions to running indoors. Not all children would feel comfortable enough to challenge an adult in this way. Just because Steven always runs and Sara always follows the rules doesn't mean that they should be treated differently when they break the same rule. This can send the unintended message that the adult cares more for one child than the other.

Young children are like mirrors; they reflect back via their own behavior what they see, hear, learn, and experience from adults. If children are immersed in an environment where yelling, hitting, and name-calling are acceptable, they will use these skills to get their needs met. Conversely, if conversation and collaboration are the tools used to manage conflict, these are the tools a child will use when conflict arises. Once children reach the developmental stage during which friends become very important and they begin to develop strong peer relationships, they become less dependent on adult interactions. Your role as a caregiver and educator of young children, then, needs to be that of a supporter, motivator, supplier, and facilitator of activities and behavioral examples that foster social competency. A key to fulfilling your role is observation. By observing how children interact with others in your program, you will know what social skills they need to work on. Once you have identified these skills, the next step is to intentionally plan activities, opportunities, and materials for children to learn and practice the skills.

A Child's Environment

The environments adults create within early care and education programs and within family homes play a large role in developing social skills in children. Child development researchers define a child's environment as the total of all things a child regularly comes in contact with. In the book *Beginnings and Beyond: Foundations in Early Childhood Education*, Ann Miles Gordon and Kathryn Williams Browne (2011) contend that children's learning environments consist of three dimensions: temporal, interpersonal, and physical. Gordon and Browne maintain that all three dimensions must be addressed to ensure the overall environment will both appeal to children and support their needs. Gordon and Browne define these three environmental dimensions as follows:

- **temporal:** schedules, routines, rules, regulations, and learning opportunities that meet children's needs

- **interpersonal:** the relationships and interactions of all individuals involved in the program, including the children, the staff, the parents, and the greater community
- **physical:** the indoor and outdoor setting, including furnishings, materials, and architectural elements of lighting, color, plumbing, and physical layout of the space

Within these three dimensions, adults need to determine how environmental elements positively or negatively influence children's ability to learn social skills. Use the following questions to help you explore how your environment encourages the building of appropriate social skills. The answers to these questions will help you define areas of strength and areas that need improvement. (Each of the following chapters will discuss strategies for supporting specific social skills within all three environmental dimensions.)

- How often do children have access to free play each day?
- How do you handle conflict?
- Does your program have step-by-step guidelines for solving conflicts? Do all staff understand and follow these guidelines?
- Does your program offer children opportunities to have a job or role?
- How do you determine what behaviors, materials, and interactions are inappropriate in your program? How is that information communicated to staff and families?
- How do your environment, activities, schedules, and intentional teaching support each of the seven social skill sets (communication, coping, community building, conflict resolution, confidence, curiosity, and control)?

A Child's Temperament

Although children are not born with social skills, they are born with specific temperaments. This book classifies children's temperaments in three ways: flexible, feisty, and fearful.

The descriptions on page 10 can help you determine what type of temperament a specific child has. However, be aware that in some situations a child with one temperament may seem to have another temperament. Temperament type can either help or hamper children in learning and retrieving specific social skills. How social skills are introduced, practiced, and supported

FLEXIBLE	FEISTY	FEARFUL
• easygoing	• highly active (but not hyperactive), inquisitive, even intense	• mostly inactive and fussy
• optimistic		• shier and more hesitant and cautious than peers
• happy	• distracted by loud noises, bright lights, food textures	• reacts negatively to new foods, people, places
• predictable		
• calm, can adjust easily to environmental factors and even radical changes	• unsure of how to react to new situations and people	• reacts more positively with continuous exposure
	• jumps right in, often creates conflict	• retreats from conflict
• able to cope with loud noises, bright lights, different food textures	• persistent when faced with a challenge	• gives up when faced with a challenge
• may resent not getting their way	• often predisposed to disruptive or aggressive behavior, exhibited in temper tantrums, excessive fussiness, or loud outbursts	• may need more time during transitions than others need
• tend to have deep feelings but show little outward emotion		• thrives when the environment (including routines, schedule, staff, and physical setting) remains constant
	• functions well with a patient, consistent approach and clearly explained boundaries	

can go a long way in helping children with challenging temperaments learn social skills. The following chapters discuss how each type of temperament affects a child's ability to learn specific skills.

The Process of Learning Social Skills

Think of social skills as a set of tools. Each tool has a specific purpose or purposes. Everyone carries a social toolbox, but not everyone—children or adults—has all the tools needed for every situation. A safe and accepting environment offers children many opportunities to add tools to their toolboxes and improve the quality of their tools. These are tools that they will use throughout their lives. When adults teach social skills and provide opportunities for children to practice these skills, children learn how to respond to problems in a way that solves rather than worsens them or creates new problems.

It may take adults some time interacting with a child or group of children to determine what skills a child has or does not have. During this assessment process, adults caring for young children may be tempted to use the same ruler to measure social competency in the children that the adult's parents used on them. But it is unfair to assume that children have had the same experiences, adult intervention, behavioral expectations, and family support the adult received when growing up. Times have changed, and environmental and social constructs have also changed. Even within the same family, children seldom develop social skills at the same rate or with the same level of success.

Wouldn't it be great if all children were socially competent? You can see this is not so at any playground, child care program, preschool, or sporting event. Children's skills reflect their surroundings and interactions. Assuming that children of a certain size or age should have specific skills or should know better than they do is a big mistake. That is not how social competency works. Children do not acquire social skills with age or through osmosis, but rather through intentional teaching, modeling, and practice. Children learn social skills while they are engaged in guided activities and independent free play in environments equipped with materials and supplies that encourage children to test their ideas about life.

Humans are social by nature. Even infants interact with other people. They turn toward a familiar voice. They smile when someone holds them. They coo when they are happy and cry when they need something. They even mimic facial expressions, such as sticking out their tongue. These social interactions help young children learn through repetition how to get their needs met. Think for a minute about a time when an infant dropped a toy from a high chair. Did you pick it up and give it back to the child? If so, the child quickly learned that you will pick up the toy when it's dropped, and it soon becomes a game. The child wants the toy. Each time the child drops the toy, you return it. The child's needs get met.

Similarly, have you ever seen a toddler reach for something you didn't want the toddler to have, so you told them no and moved the item away, then the child moved toward the item and reached for it again? How you reacted to the repeat attempt taught the toddler a lot about what was appropriate and what was not. Toddlers learn to read body cues such as facial expressions. So if you laughed, you made it a game. If you frowned, then you sent a message that the child's behavior was not OK. Even without words, your message was clear. The child gained information from these interactions and stored it for use in similar future situations.

As children grow, their vocabulary and small- and large-muscle groups develop, and they begin to mimic how others solve problems. Toddlers and preschoolers may see a child hit or bite another child to get a desired toy. If the hitting or biting child is successful, then the watching child stores that information for future use.

You may hear children using inappropriate language or hurtful words and be aghast. Try to remember that children do not make up these words. They are repeating what they have heard others say in similar situations to get a familiar reaction. Often children do not even know what the words mean. Respond with something like "In our program, we do not use that language. It is hurtful to others, and everyone is safe here." Sometimes the child will retort, "I am allowed to use that word at home," or "My parents use that word." Avoid a tug-of-war by saying, "What is said at home is between you and your parents. I need to keep everyone safe here, and so those words are not allowed." Follow up by asking the child what else they could have said. That type of question helps the child identify words that are appropriate for the program and convey their intended message. It also helps the child add appropriate words to their vocabulary that convey a certain emotion or level of frustration. This places the child in the role of problem solver rather than problem maker.

Children grow and develop both physically and cognitively in a predictable sequence; however, they do not achieve mastery at the exact same age as their siblings or their same-age peers. Some children excel in a particular area while others lag in the same area, even if they are in the same family or taught by the same teacher. Children are unique individuals who grow and develop interests and areas of mastery in unique ways. It is through observation and trial and error that children develop their social skills. First they gather information by observing how others solve their problems, become engaged in social situations, or get what they want. Then they will use the information (social tool) gained to get what they want—to enter a playgroup, get the last building block, or get a yellow crayon from a friend. Once they have used a tool, they will evaluate how successful it was at achieving their goal.

THE BENEFITS OF TEACHING POSITIVE SOCIAL SKILLS

The Center on the Social and Emotional Foundations for Early Learning (CSEFEL) states, "Research has shown that children who can interact successfully with their peers, even during preschool, are more popular, have stronger friendships, and are included more often in classroom activities than children who lack these skills" (accessed 2018). An article published in the scientific journal *Child Development* asserts that intentionally teaching social skills increased social competence in recognizing emotions, developing empathy, making and keeping friends, and making good choices (Taylor et al. 2017). When children need help and feel confident enough to approach an adult and ask for help, they have a better chance of successfully completing a given task. It is the social skills of confidence and communication that help the child seek help when needed. If children do not have these skills, they will use other skills that could be disruptive to the learning environment to deflect attention from their lack of skills or their inability to complete a task.

Positive social skills play a large role in determining how well children will do in school and in developing lasting relationships. When children are welcoming to others, have empathy, and are willing to collaborate with others, they often have more friends than children who do not have these skills. When children can accept others for who they are, this allows them to find and keep friends. Good communication skills allow children to express their needs and wants effectively while respecting the rights and opinions of others and can help a child traverse the day-to-day challenges of school and life. Learning to follow the rules, accept responsibility, delay gratification, and handle competition and disappointment in an appropriate way provides a framework to negotiate the demands of school. The social skills of problem solving and impulse control allow children to stop and think about the results of certain actions. Children who have these skills are less likely to choose risky behaviors than children who do not have these skills.

THE BENEFITS OF PLAY

Adults may look at children's play as time spent in frivolous activity without any intentionality or direct learning, but the reality is that play helps support school success by developing social skills in children. It is often said that play is the child's work. It is through this work that children learn about their world and how to function in it. Play is so important to the healthy development of a child that the United Nations recognizes play as a right deserved by every child (UN Human Rights 1990, Article 31.1).

Zero to Three is a nonprofit organization devoted to improving the lives of very young children. According to Zero to Three (2004), "Play is fun and important to young children's intellectual, social, emotional, and physical development. Through play, children learn problem-solving, interpersonal skills, communication, and other skills integral to success in school and life." Play supports children's overall health by stimulating their curiosity, building positive relationships, and improving physical development. Play comes in all forms—from playing catch, to playing a board game with friends, to dressing up, to running cars on a track, to making up a song, to acting out a situation in dramatic play. All of these situations and many more provide time for children to make sense of the world around them.

Creating opportunities for unscheduled play experiences encourages children to wonder how things work and test what they already know. This open-ended playtime allows children to think outside the box and create new things from old or modify playthings to meet a specific need. Encouraging children to problem solve during play helps children learn that they can figure things out for themselves. Adults are often too quick to "fix it" for children rather than asking guided questions to help a child come up with a solution. Clarify with children what they are trying to accomplish in order to offer suggestions and supplies that may achieve the child's end goal. Then ask some questions to put the children in the driver's seat, such as the following:

- "What have you already tried?"
- "What else do you think you could try next?"
- "Can you think of another way to do that?"
- "What else would you need to make that happen?"
- "Since we do not have that, what else can you use?"

An adult once asked a child, "What is play?" They said, "It is what I do when someone is not telling me to do something." During play, children have opportunities to choose whom they would like to play with and what they would like to do. It is through these interactions with others that children develop friendships. They soon learn through trial and error what they like about others and what they do not like. They learn the traits of a good friend and how to treat others so that others will play with them. Like adults, children need and want friends. Friendships are important in the lives of children. Friends provide a safe place for children to share things about themselves. Friends are there for each other even if they do not agree. Through friendship children learn important social skills, such as collaboration, negotiation, empathy, and effective communication, that will serve them well as they grow into adulthood.

Play fosters physical development in children. For example, small-motor development occurs when a child is stringing beads, holding a pencil, or putting a puzzle together. Hand-eye coordination happens when children are placing items in a basket, coloring, weaving a place mat, or painting at an easel. Large-motor development occurs when children are dancing to music, playing baseball, running relay races, or throwing a ball. Play activities can work specific muscle groups or multiple muscle groups. A variety of large- and small-motor activities both indoors and outdoors help children develop and strengthen all their muscle groups and grow physically. When you are planning these activities, take into consideration the children's current skill levels. For instance, it is hard to play catch if you have never thrown a ball, or to do a skipping relay race if you have never been taught to skip.

Among the many types of physical development fostered by play is brain development. On NPR's *Morning Edition*, Sergio Pellis, a researcher from the University of Lethbridge in Alberta, Canada, explained, "The experience of play changes the connections of the neurons at the front end of your brain. . . . And without play experience, those neurons aren't changed." Pellis contended that those changes help wire brains for executive function, which plays an essential role in plan making, emotion control, and problem solving. Jaak Panksepp, at Washington State University, added, "The function of play is to build pro-social brains, social brains that know how to interact with others in positive ways" (Hamilton 2014).

These modern views on the value of play dovetail with the theories of earlier developmental psychologists, such as Jean Piaget and Lev Vygotsky. Piaget contended that through play, children have opportunities to obtain knowledge about the world around them. They create stories and elaborate on old ones, helping them to practice social skills and understand situations that are a part of their world (Piaget [1951] 2013). Vygotsky asserted that play provides opportunities for children to develop emotional and self-regulation skills. He said, "A child's play is not simply a reproduction of what he has experienced, but a creative reworking of the impressions he has acquired. He combines them and uses them to construct a new reality, one that conforms to his own needs and desires" (Vygotsky 1967).

Engaging children in play opportunities that teach social skills and support social skills development can help children work out the social interactions within their peer group. The process of play can be the venue for building effective and appropriate communication skills. Children use different skills when they engage in different interest areas and with different peers. Play allows time to engage in problem solving and collaboration between children and within groups. It is through play that children learn coping skills, negotiation, and conflict resolution.

As children play with others and do not get their way or get a turn, they learn how to handle disappointment by developing appropriate coping skills. Negotiation and problem solving occur during play as children talk about how to play a game, who is going first, who stacked their blocks so they do not fall down, or who can get their car to go farther. Whenever children get together in a group, disagreements are bound to occur. Adults typically jump in to settle the disagreements—but when they do this, they thwart an opportunity for the children to learn how to link behaviors, feelings, and emotions to body language and words. It is important to let the children learn to work it out and communicate with one another.

PROVIDERS' ROLE

Today's families are busy with multiple jobs, schedules, meetings, to-do lists, children's extracurricular activities, and more. It can be hard for family members to plan unscheduled time for children to just play. So the first and most important step for child care providers is to provide in their programs what families might not be able to provide at home: unfettered playtimes and environments that support imaginative play. In organized early childhood care and education programs, free play is usually offered daily, and outdoor play is required as long as weather permits. Free play can be anything from shared reading to taking a walk, from playing a board game to making a tent under the table. Children involved in free play find their voice and learn to share their ideas and collaborate with others. As children grow and change, so does their play. Mimicking daily life might be perfect for toddlers and preschoolers; however, school-age children like to take on multiple roles and challenges using higher-level thinking and problem solving. It is important to let the children play in their own way so they can develop scenarios that are important to them while allowing them to work through problems or expand their knowledge of a topic or event. Above all, children need time to be children and leave behind whatever stressors exist in their lives for a little while. Being engaged in the process of exploration and skill building helps children de-stress, regroup, and face life again. Here are some tips to encourage free play:

- If you don't like mess, use mess-reducing strategies, thereby reducing your stress.
- Engage in conversation with children about their play.
- Plan enough time for children to become engaged.
- Provide toys that have more than one purpose.
- Provide space that allows children to expand play over time.
- Add nontraditional activities and materials, such as woodworking and take-apart art, to your play space.
- When children ask, provide materials or supplies to extend or support an activity.
- Change the environment when children have lost interest in it.

Create environments that encourage children to play in groups. Try to find time to play with children. This might seem overwhelming when you are managing several children in the same space, but the benefits can be numerous. Playing side by side with children offers the chance to engage in conversation and can provide information about what the children like and what issues they are having. Sometimes a teacher playing with children encourages reluctant children to join in the play. It also can create opportunities for children to make new friends. In addition, rotating around the room when the children are in free play can help you identify areas that children are not using so that you can add or change materials to encourage interest in those areas again.

Plan for both indoor and outdoor free time, because each environment provides different benefits to help children grow. While indoors may provide a greater variety of activities and materials, outdoors provides space for large-motor activities alongside quiet places to relax. Large-motor activities, such as relay races, tag, and hide-and-seek, can be easily implemented within any outdoor play space. Offering children the option to read a book on a blanket under a tree, draw a picture with chalk on the pavement, or play checkers with a friend gives children the option to de-stress and simply relax and enjoy the outdoors.

Find out what children are interested in. Use group time to generate a list of ideas for play spaces. Children are more likely to engage in imaginative play when it is based on their own interest and input. Within each play space, allow the children to take the lead to encourage creativity. Provide additional resources when requested or needed to encourage their creativity. Children may need some guidance or an introduction to the theme of a play area, so be prepared to give it, but be ready to back out of play when the children are engaged.

As children traverse through play spaces, they will soon demonstrate which social skills they have and which they lack. Some social deficits may be easy to spot, such as a child who hits in frustration, while others are harder to identify, such as a child who is always watching a playgroup but never engages in it. So begin by observing and documenting what a child does well and does not do well within a given interaction. Remember to note both the positive and the negative. For example, you may find that a child successfully entered a play situation, asked for a crayon, or defused a conflict with peers without adult intervention. These are all good things to document and remember when another conflict arises. When children demonstrate good social skills, acknowledge what they said or did that you would like them to repeat. For example, say, "The words you used really helped TaySean feel better," or "That made Anna feel less frustrated when you helped her put away the blocks. You acted like a good friend." Such simple, specific statements tell children exactly what they did that was helpful. Children can take pride in their good choices while adding social skills to their toolbox for future use in similar situations.

Children are seldom 100 percent successful, because there are so many variables at play—such as different children, changes in the environment, lack of materials, stress, or health issues—and these change constantly. Each variable can affect the outcome of an interaction. It is important for both parents and providers to remember that just because a child handled a situation well yesterday, that doesn't guarantee success today. One-time success does not mean mastery. Help a child be successful by talking through the situation and encouraging the child to generate other strategies that might work next time. Record what you saw, and be specific. Take time to find out the entire story from all parties involved to get a clear picture of the events leading up to the incident. When you are documenting a conflict, ask yourself the following questions (for a reproducible copy of these questions, see appendix A):

- Where did the observation happen? Indoors or outdoors?
- In what area of the indoor or outdoor space did the observation occur?
- Who was involved?
- What time of day was it?
- What happened to cause the conflict? Describe the event using children's names, and quote their conversations.
- Do these children usually play well together?

- Were the children taking turns talking to one another, or were they talking over one another during the conflict? Explain, using quotes.
- Was there pushing, shoving, or hitting?
- Did a child get hurt? Was an incident report filed?
- Was there name-calling?
- Were the children taking turns explaining what happened when discussing the problem with an adult?
- Did the environment have enough supplies and materials for all the children to play successfully?
- Was a separate place available where the children could go to problem solve and discuss this situation?
- Who solved the problem, the children or the adult?
- Were the children in conflict able to rejoin play successfully?

You might wonder why you should note the time of day and the location of a conflict. Determining if there are certain times of the day and areas of the room where conflict occurs more frequently is important. This information helps you determine if a pattern exists. If a pattern does exist, then you can take steps to minimize conflict in the future. For example, if conflict tends to occur with a specific child before lunch, then maybe the child is hungry, has low blood sugar, or is ready for a nap. If conflict always happens in the art area, then maybe you have too few or too many supplies in the area, or too many children are allowed in the area given the available furniture and supplies.

Once a skill deficit has been identified, a family member and provider can outline a plan to work on skills both at home and in the classroom. This should start with a conversation about things already done—and things that could be done—at home and in the program to help the child learn a specific skill. This conversation will create a supportive, stable learning system to benefit the child. Being consistent through all a child's environments about the approach to developing specific social skills sends a clear message to the child about how to deal with a particular problem.

In the following scenario, the teacher was across the room, and loud voices drew her to the block area. She moved closer to view what was happening and to see if the children could solve the problem on their own.

The children had just returned from outdoor play and went into free-choice time. Sara and Tyrone were playing with blocks. A third child, Anne, entered their space and began taking blocks to build her own tower.

Sara said, "No, those are my blocks!"

Tyrone said, "Give them back! We are playing here."

Anne grabbed several blocks and started walking away. As she left, she knocked down the tower Sara and Tyrone were building. Tyrone followed Anne, but rather than grab the blocks from her, he went to the teacher and asked for help.

The teacher called Sara over to the group. She asked both Sara and Tyrone to explain what happened. Anne talked over the other children, so the teacher calmly reminded her to listen and then she would have her turn. When it was Anne's turn to talk, she explained that she wanted to play with Sara and Tyrone, and they wouldn't let her and she was mad.

The teacher prompted her by saying, "Is that why you knocked down the tower?"

Anne said, "Yes."

The teacher asked Anne how she would feel if she worked really hard on a tower and someone knocked it down. She reminded Anne of when she worked on her picture at the art table the day before and another child ripped it up. The teacher asked Anne, "How did that make you feel?" Connecting the events of the current conflict with those from Anne's own past helped Anne understand Sara's and Tyrone's feelings and develop empathy.

Let's analyze this situation by answering the questions outlined earlier:

- Where did the observation happen? Indoors or outdoors?
  Indoors.
- In what area of the indoor or outdoor space did the observation occur?
  The block area.
- Who was involved?
  Tyrone, Anne, and Sara. They do not usually play together.

Chapter 1

- What time of day was it?

  Just after outdoor time.

- What happened to cause the conflict? Describe the event using children's names, and quote their conversations.

  Sara and Tyrone were playing in the block area, building towers and buildings with blocks. A third child (Anne) came into the block space and wanted to play but did not know how to enter the group and play with children already there, so instead she took the blocks from Sara and Tyrone, then knocked down their blocks when they did not accept her into the group.

- Do these children usually play well together?

  Sometimes, not often.

- Were the children taking turns talking to one another, or were they talking over one another during the conflict? Explain, using quotes.

  They were yelling at one another. Sara: "No, those are my blocks!" Tyrone: "Give them back! We are playing here."

- Was there pushing, shoving, or hitting?

  No, but Anne knocked down the other children's tower and took blocks from the area.

- Did a child get hurt? Was an incident report filed?

  No one got hurt; no incident report was filed.

- Was there name-calling?

  No.

- Were the children taking turns explaining what happened when discussing the problem with an adult?

  Anne had a difficult time listening to Sara and Tyrone. She tried to talk over them and correct them midsentence. I had to remind her that she would have her time to talk, but she needed to listen first.

- Did the environment have enough supplies and materials for all the children to play successfully?

  No.

- Was a separate place available where the children could go to problem solve and discuss this situation?

  No.

- Who solved the problem, the children or the adult?

  The adult acted as a facilitator.

- Were the children in conflict able to rejoin play successfully?
  Anne was too upset to go to the block area and chose the art area instead. She worked alongside other children without further incident. Sara and Tyrone returned to the block area and continued playing without further incident.

Here's what we can learn from this analysis:

- **Skills possessed:** Sara and Tyrone were assertive. They expressed to Anne why she could not have the blocks. Both Tyrone and Sara were able to remain under control even when their tower was knocked down. Tyrone chose to seek help from the teacher rather than struggle to get the blocks back from Anne.
- **Skills lacking:** Anne did not understand how to enter a playgroup successfully. Tyrone and Sara had not learned how to problem solve on their own. Anne exhibited lack of control and lack of empathy when she knocked down the tower. All the children needed help with communication skills. The children had a hard time taking turns listening and talking about what happened.
- **Environmental supports:** Staff were available to step in if children could not solve the problem themselves. Staff were trained in conflict resolution.
- **Environmental deficit:** The space did not have a visual limitation on the block area, such as a picture of two children posted at the entrance to the space so children could self-manage occupancy. The space was not equipped with enough materials for all interested children to play. The classroom lacked a quiet space to talk to the children or problem solve together or for the children to calm down before acting out.

Equipped with this information, the adult will need to intentionally plan activities for the children to practice communication skills. Helping the children role-play how to enter a playgroup or how to ask for a toy from another child helps establish ground rules for effective communication, such as taking turns listening and talking. Discussing with the children how they would feel if a child tore their paper or took their toy helps develop empathy by linking a previous event that generated the same feeling to the current event. Role play can be a great addition to group time. The adult will need to determine if the children need help managing occupancy of the block area. If they do need help, the adult can post a visual representation of the number of children allowed in that area or add more supplies to accommodate more than two children in the block area.

Play provides ongoing opportunities for children to learn coping, negotiation, problem-solving, and communication skills. For example, as children talk about how to play a game, who is going first, or how to stack their blocks so they do not fall down, you can teach negotiation and problem-solving skills. Taking turns and learning how to handle disappointment during play helps children develop coping skills. Children often act impulsively or inappropriately because they feel that no one understands them or is listening to them. Children gain skills and strategies from watching familiar and trusted adults handle difficult situations. Making it clear that your program is a safe place and that certain words and behaviors are not acceptable will help children understand when you are requesting that they choose other words or different behaviors. Once you have helped children process an inappropriate event, it's time to talk about other ways to handle the situation as well as other words they could have used. This gives them tools to use if a similar situation arises in the future. When you see children starting to make an inappropriate choice, offer an opportunity to make a different choice. This offer lets them know that what they are about to do is unacceptable in your program and allows them to take control of their behavior and make a more appropriate choice. Not all children will take the hint at first, but when this process is used consistently, children become familiar with it. Each time you allow children to make a different choice, you send the message that you believe they *can* come up with an appropriate choice. Sometimes all children need is to know that someone believes in their ability to choose appropriately.

Communication

WHAT IS COMMUNICATION?

Communication occurs in a variety of ways. Simply defined, *communication* is the exchange of information. People exchange information through verbal, nonverbal, and written means. This chapter focuses mainly on verbal and non-verbal communication, which are the means most often used by young children.

Verbal Communication

Verbal communication involves both talking and listening. Long before infants can talk, they can hear and recognize words as labels for things, such as a pacifier or a comfort toy. Older infants and young toddlers begin to play with sound and start to assign words to familiar items, such as a *bottle* or *blanket*. Older toddlers understand and use more and more words over time. The average two-year-old understands approximately two hundred words but uses only fifty words routinely.

Young children can be very egocentric. They are more concerned with what they want or need than with the needs of others. It does not even occur to them to look beyond what they themselves want. This egocentrism plays a role in how they learn to communicate.

As young children learn to communicate, the subject matter usually centers on their own wants and needs. Young toddlers may point to a wanted item, rather than use words, because a toddler either has not been taught the needed word or does not remember it. In the midst of a busy day, it may seem easier or more practical to just give the item to the child. But in the long run, this approach limits the child's vocabulary. Adults need to tell young children the words for items so that in the future the children will use those words and become more successful at getting what they want.

Older toddlers and young preschoolers are very adamant about what they want you to do or where they would like you to sit. Each encounter with adults can provide teachable moments so children can increase their vocabulary and label their emotions. When they are expressing their needs, they can learn words for their frustration, such as *mad* or *sad*. In addition, they can learn appropriate words to ask for things they want or to explain why they want an adult to do a specific task.

Preschoolers and young schoolagers love to talk, especially to adults. They are willing to talk about almost anything. However, these children seldom understand that communication is a two-way street; it includes not only sending but also receiving information. Often children are so involved in telling their story that they do not stop to listen to the other person's point of view. As a result, they miss information and become frustrated or confused about how others respond to them. This sort of conversation meets children's need to be heard, but it doesn't help them learn how to listen when others talk. Children need help from adults to develop listening skills.

First, adults need to watch children as they experience daily events and situations. This observation can show parents and providers how appropriately or inappropriately children respond during conversations. Then adults need to intentionally teach listening skills to help children understand that communication is a two-way street. First, you have to get children's attention. You can do this by making eye contact, holding their hand, or going to a quiet place free from distractions to talk. Once you have their attention, talk directly to them and give them your full attention when they are talking. This models how a two-way conversation happens. Have children repeat back what they heard to make sure they understood the full intended message. Playing a game of telephone is a great way to help children see how messages can change as they pass from one person to another. These techniques can help a child understand how important it is to both talk and listen to others when you are communicating with them.

Nonverbal Communication

When we think about communication, we often think first of verbal communication. We might forget—or not even realize—that nonverbal messages often communicate part of our message long before we've spoken a word. During any communication process, both parties send nonverbal clues through body language.

Body language is the silent message your body sends to others within a discussion. It tells how you feel about the topic of the conversation or a person within the conversation. You send such messages via facial expressions like smiling or frowning, gestures like rolling your eyes or clenching your hands, and tone of voice. Body language adds another dimension to a conversation. It strengthens the overall communication by linking the verbal message with the emotion(s) surrounding the message.

Reading body language helps people determine the meaning other people are trying to communicate. But often people are so caught up in their own messages that they don't see the body language messages of others. Adults often choose not to see others' body language. Young children, however, simply may not know how to read it.

Modeling nonverbal communication helps children learn how to become mentally and physically engaged in a conversation and effectively convey and receive messages. Making eye contact and giving children your complete attention, even if you have to leave the room to talk, tells them that you are interested in what they have to say. Talking in a calm voice while smiling sends children the message that you care for them. Holding a child's hand during a conversation helps the child focus on what you are saying and shows that you are engaged in the conversation.

Written Communication

As children get older and start learning to read and write, written communication becomes another way in which they communicate. As children move from preschool to elementary school, they begin to put their own words on paper. In the beginning, they may spell words phonetically, leaving the reader mystified as to the meaning. As they continue learning to write, they often use fragmented sentences that do not convey a complete thought. When adults scribe children's words, such as describing pictures they have drawn, they show children how to put their words together to tell a story. Over time and with practice, children can learn to consistently convey their intended message to the reader. Adults who encourage children to write down their stories or encourage journal writing help children become masters of the written word.

Digital Communication

Digital communication involves a combination of verbal, nonverbal, and written communication. Young children communicate with others via many types of digital media, such as video chat, games, and other applications loaded on smartphones, tablets, and computers. Even infants use digital communication when their families and caregivers engage them in video chatting. Adults often use video chat to connect with their children while away from them, or to connect children with extended family members who live far away. This type of communication can help children learn how to participate in verbal conversations and how to read facial cues.

Digital communication is pervasive in modern American daily life. According to a 2013 Common Sense Media report, "The only way to maximize the positive impact—and minimize the negative—is to have an accurate understanding of the role it plays in their lives." This report explains that 75 percent of children ages zero through eight have access to some type of mobile device at home, such as a smartphone or tablet. It continues, "Of the roughly two hours (1:55) average screen media use each day, half (50%) is spent watching television on a TV set (:57). This compares to 19% spent watching DVDs, 13% using mobile devices, 10% using computers, and 9% using video game players" (Common Sense Media 2013).

It is rare to see families together in public without one or more family members using digital media. Adults often give young children smartphones or tablets so they can view a video or play a game when dining out, shopping, and riding in the car. Toddlers and preschoolers can easily find and use the apps they like without adult intervention. This type of communication can give children information that may or may not be appropriate for them.

As children enter elementary school, their access to digital communication expands. Children may receive smartphones, laptops, and tablets of their own. Throughout the school years (including kindergarten), many children are using digital media in the classroom, to turn in assignments, at home to practice skills and expand on information taught at school, and to communicate with teachers and peers. Some classrooms are creating dedicated online social meeting space and providing access only to those students within the classroom. In the middle grades, children may begin sending written messages to others via email, texting, and social media. Written communication in the digital world can be faceless and nameless. Children may say things that are hurtful and unkind, or even dangerous, without realizing the consequences or understanding how their messages are received.

According to Dr. Yolanda Reid Chassiakos and Dr. Corinn Cross's presentation "Young Minds and Media," in 1971 the average age at which children started watching television was four years old. But they say, "Today, children begin to interact with digital media as early as *four months* of age." They further report the new norm is that "at age four, half of children had their own television and three-fourths had their own mobile device." They contend that nearly 97 percent of all children use mobile devices, and most started using them before twelve months (Reid Chassiakos and Cross 2017).

The American Academy of Pediatrics (AAP) recommends that "for children younger than eighteen months, avoid use of screen media other than video-chatting." The AAP also recommends limiting screen time to one hour per day for children ages two to five years old, and that time should consist of high-quality programming. For older children, the AAP encourages adults to "place consistent limits on the time spent using media, and the types of media, and make sure media does not take the place of adequate sleep, physical activity and other behaviors essential to health" (2016).

Parents and caregivers should review each digital platform, app, and website children use at school, child care programs, and home. Make use of any parental controls available for the devices that children use. Check with your internet and mobile phone providers to see if you can track where children go when they are online and while using mobile phones. Teach children that all of their online activities leave digital footprints, and that once a digital message has been sent, there is no taking it back.

ASSOCIATED SKILLS

Expressing Feelings

Emotions are part and parcel of children's lives. Children's emotions can change quickly: one minute they are happy, and the next minute they are angry. Dealing with children's emotions can be daunting. We may not understand why children feel a certain way; however, their feelings are valid and important. Emotions—such as anger, frustration, confusion, excitement, fear, and boredom—can alter how children respond to a situation or topic and how children communicate with others. For example, when strong emotions are in play, often children do not hear others.

Because we cannot delve into other people and feel what they are feeling at any specific moment, it is wise to take time to observe children's behavior and try to understand their emotions. You could then say, "It seems as though you are feeling very _____." This statement allows children to correct you if you've guessed wrong, so that you are on the same page going forward. Such statements also give children a chance to self-identify their feelings. Learning to label their feelings helps children manage those feelings.

Children need to learn how to express their feelings while being respectful of others, even if they have hurt feelings or are angry. Controlling their emotions is an important communication skill. Acting upset and combative during a conversation takes attention away from the message and focuses attention on the behavior. When attention shifts in this way, children may feel that they are not being heard. This can accelerate the problematic behavior and derail the conversation. Therefore, the first step in teaching children how to express their emotions is helping them learn to self-soothe or calm themselves down when they're frustrated or angry.

Infants cry when they are uncomfortable. They need your attention when they cry. In addition, helping them learn to soothe themselves at an early age can create long-term benefits for the child. Children can soothe themselves in a variety of ways. Infants can suck on a pacifier. Toddlers may suck their thumb or rub the edge of a blanket. Preschoolers may hug a stuffed animal or curl their hair with their finger. Schoolagers may listen to music or read a book. Children of any age may want to be sung to, may want to have their back or arms rubbed, or may need to move their bodies by rocking back and forth. Regardless of the method, the ultimate goal is to help children find ways to self-soothe. The ability to get themselves under control prior to or during a conversation is important in effectively voicing their point of view and hearing the point of view of others.

Toddlers have very little self-control. They want what they want and see no reason they cannot have it. Often toddlers have a limited word bank, and they can become frustrated easily because they have a hard time making themselves understood. Toddlers believe themselves able to do things older children can do, and they may become incensed when they are not able or not allowed to do these things. Not allowing toddlers to do unsafe activities can cause a tug-of-war between the adult and child; toddlers simply do not understand why they cannot do what they want. Toddlers are very demanding and distractible. They do not express their emotions in words, but rather in actions. Temper tantrums are common in toddlers because of their limited ability to express what they want and their frustration at not being understood.

As toddlers begin to verbalize, they play with sounds and repeat words they have heard. Toddlers sometimes point at the things they want. They may not know the correct way to ask for something; all they know is that they want it. When they are given that item, children learn that pointing is an easy strategy to use for getting what they want. If adults do not teach children how to ask for something, they will continue to point or use single-word demands, such as "Cookie!" or "Bottle!" For instance, if children extend their arms, wanting you to pick them up, you could use the opportunity to ask, "Do you want me to pick you up?" You may need to prompt children to say, "Up, please."

Adults teaching children the words they need to use to get their needs met is important. If adults use baby talk, some children will mimic them instead of using correct terms for items. While primary caregivers may know what children are asking for when they use baby talk or gestures, others may not—leaving children frustrated at not being understood. Talk to the children in your care as they are doing everyday tasks and activities, such as playing with a ball, getting dressed, or taking a bath. Describe what they are doing, such as saying, "You are taking a bath," or "Let's put socks on your feet." Frequently use the names of children's favorite things, because children are more likely to join in conversation if it involves something they like. Place a favorite item just out of children's reach and have them request the item, such as by saying, "Car, please." Over time you can increase the amount of words to "May I please have my _____." With repetition and patience, you can create stepping-stones for children to successfully get the desired item.

The goal for parents and providers is to help children learn words, express their feelings, and get their needs met appropriately. The key for adults is consistency; if a behavior is not OK today, then it needs to be not OK tomorrow too. Multiple adults caring for the same child must agree on the rules of a child's life, because it does not take long for children to figure out whom to go to to get what they want.

For most preschoolers, vocabulary grows from 900–1,000 words at age three to 1,500–1,600 words by age four. Despite this vocabulary growth, children do not always know what to say to someone who has wronged them, such as by taking a toy, hitting them, or calling them names. Preschool-age children want to play with others but still believe, like toddlers, that they should always get what they want—so play is not always easy. When preschoolers feel that they are right and others are wrong, or when they can't do or have something they want, they can be stubborn. If they do not get their way, they may display strong feelings in a variety of ways. Expressing their feelings appropriately can be difficult. They may cry, shout, push, and shove to let others know how they feel. Adults must continue to encourage children of preschool age to use words rather than inappropriate behavior to solve their problems. Sometimes the adult needs to provide the words and encourage children to speak those words to other children. This approach helps children learn the correct words to say and remember these words for another time. The following scenario offers an example of this strategy.

Seven children sat on the floor while the teacher read them a book. As the children listened, one child, Pam, crawled over another child, Shelly.

Shelly said, "Pam!"

Pam said, "What?"

Shelly looked at the teacher for help.

The teacher said to Shelly, "Tell her you do not like it when she crawls over you."

Shelly then said, "Pam, I do not like it when you crawl over me, and that hurt."

Pam said, "OK." She moved and sat next to Shelly. The girls continued to sit side by side as the teacher finished reading the story.

When Shelly looked to the teacher for help, rather than speak for Shelly, the teacher told her what words to say and encouraged her to say the words. This process gave Shelly a vocabulary to use, then empowered her to tell Pam that she did not like being crawled over. The teacher sent the message that she believed Shelly could handle this problem herself. The teacher could have just told Pam not to crawl over other children, but that would have sent the message that the teacher would solve all the children's problems, rather than a message that the teacher believed in the children's ability to handle their own conflicts. For every child, there will come a time when a problem happens and an adult is not present, so children need to know how to solve their own problems appropriately and effectively.

Preschoolers' feelings change from minute to minute throughout the day. Things happen that adults see and do not see, and these happenings change how children feel. To help students express their feelings, one classroom used individual tabletop "feelings barometers." Every child had a milk-jug cap with his or her picture glued inside it and a piece of Velcro glued on the other side of the cap. Each child also had a piece of oaktag divided into four different-colored squares. Each color stood for a different emotion, such as red for mad, blue for sad, yellow for happy, and purple for excited. The children could move their face to the emotion they were feeling at that moment. The teacher encouraged the children to move their faces whenever their feelings changed. This strategy offered the teacher a quick, easy way to know how a child felt and helped the teacher avert meltdowns and altercations. It also helped the children self-identify and name their feelings. Another way children can identify their emotions and the strength of those emotions is to use red, blue, yellow, and purple color-gradient paint chips. By pointing to a particular shade of red or yellow, children can tell adults how upset or happy they are. The adult can then suggest individualized strategies to cope with each of the four feelings.

A typical six-year-old child can say 2,600 words but understands about 20,000 words, and vocabulary increases at a rate of six to seven words per day. Children ages eight to twelve learn approximately twelve words per day. School-age children like to hold conversations with adults and peers alike, and they have diverse interests and like to stay busy. They like to please adults and will mimic adult behavior. They are beginning to understand others' perspectives and feelings, which helps them solve problems without adult intervention. They have a concrete sense of right and wrong. When someone opposes a child's sense of right and wrong, emotions can surface that can cause arguments, emotional outbursts, and hurt feelings. Helping children to identify and manage their emotions can set the stage for understanding others' points of view.

Friendships are important to school-age children. In the primary grades, children tend to have same-gender friend groups, while in the middle grades, mixed-gender friend groups become the norm. Within any relationship, feelings about friends can change based on who was picked for a game or asked to come over for a playdate. Children make judgments when they feel slighted, and their feelings will often bubble up, causing them to act out in inappropriate ways. Learning to calm down and express their feelings appropriately while listening to others' points of view is an important step in maintaining friendships.

Reading Body Language

For the first year of their lives, infants use body language to communicate their wants and needs to others (Driver 2011). Infants communicate using eye contact, coos, smiles, and crying to let others know how they are feeling. Infants also use several other nonverbal cues to communicate with others. The startle reflex, also called the Moro reflex, indicates that the infant may be fearful and needs to be reassured or consoled. Babies who turn their heads away from persons or events might be saying they are bored or finished watching the event. When infants rub their eyes, they are signaling that they are tired. When babies rub their ears, they may need to be comforted. Each of these body language messages helps adults understand babies' needs and provide the appropriate support.

Toddlers often send nonverbal messages. For example, they may cross their arms when they are frightened by too much commotion or by a new toy they do not understand. They may cover their heads when they are unsure about a new person or place. Some toddlers may run away when an adult comes to play with them or help them with a task, indicating that they are big now and can do it themselves. Toddlers may avert their eyes when you come to check on them when they've been unusually quiet, communicating that they did something wrong and that they are sorry. They can read facial expressions and know when a person is happy or sad. Even though toddlers are beginning to use words, body language is a very important tool in sending and decoding messages.

Preschoolers and schoolagers depend more on spoken words and less on nonverbal cues. Many preschool and school-age programs use feelings charts that help children assign emotion words to facial expressions. It is also a good idea for adults to take time to observe, understand, and document how individual children's faces look when they are experiencing different feelings. Children may have different facial expressions for anger, sadness, and frustration, just as they may have different facial expressions for happiness, excitement, and fear. Adults can take pictures of children's faces after asking them, "What does your face look like when you are happy/sad/mad/excited?" These same faces can be used in a game in which children match faces showing similar emotions. This game can help children see how they and their peers look when they are happy or sad, and provide an opportunity to see different faces for the same emotions.

Adults can help children understand nonverbal communication by modeling and role-playing nonverbal cues. Children look to the caring adults in their lives to learn how to be caring during a conversation with another person. To help children identify the body language messages people are sending without words getting in the way, turn off the sound when you are watching a video or a TV program, or take your child people-watching.

Listening

While humans may be equipped with two ears for hearing, often we do not listen. Hearing is the ability to identify sound. Listening means paying attention to what is being said, in order to understand the content and respond appropriately. We hear lots of conversations, but listening closely enough for accurate understanding is a whole different ball game.

Environment and emotions can block how well we are able to listen at any given time. How many times have you been in a conversation during which you couldn't have cared less about the topic, because your mind was on whatever activity you left to have this conversation? This happens with children too. Listening is difficult for children when they really want to do something else or they really want someone to know how they feel. Perhaps they have just left a favorite play activity, are waiting to go outdoors, or are hungry and eager for lunch.

Adults often are confused as to why children don't do as they're asked right away or without several reminders. Chances are, children's minds are engaged elsewhere. To help children be successful listeners when they are in conversations, be sure to make eye contact with them or hold their hand. This will help you make sure they are listening. Have children parrot back what you said so you can make sure they heard all the information you shared.

Listening skills take time to learn and even longer to master. To alert children that it is their turn to listen, have the speaker hold an object, such as a stuffed bear or a ball. Adults should do this as well when they are speaking, so children learn to listen consistently whenever they spot the listening cue. When it's someone else's turn to speak, that person holds the bear, ball, or other object. Visual cues like this can make a big difference in establishing good listening skills. Such visual aids can be used at group time, while eating a meal, or between children who are in conflict to prevent people from talking over one another.

Assertiveness

This book defines *assertive communication* as standing up for one's own rights, beliefs, and feelings without trampling on the rights, beliefs, and feelings of others. People communicate using four basic styles: assertive, aggressive, passive, and passive aggressive. Aggressive communication is threatening; the communicator does not care about the rights of others and tends to bully others. Passive communication is compliant; the communicator avoids conflict and focuses on pleasing others, even at the cost of their own rights, beliefs, or feelings. Passive-aggressive communication is a style in which communicators use subtle insults to convey their anger or dislike of a person or thing. Each communication style affects aggression in its own way, as outlined in the following chart.

COMMUNICATION STYLE	EFFECT ON AGGRESSION
• Passivity	• Invites aggression
• Aggression	• Causes aggression
• Passive aggression	• Encourages aggression
• Assertiveness	• Dispels aggression

Being on the receiving end of passive, aggressive, or passive-aggressive communication can leave children feeling fearful, confused, and insulted. These feelings can lead children to strike back with hurtful words or physical harm. These three communication styles are not winning styles for anyone. Be sure to lead children away from these styles when you see them demonstrated, because they do not allow children to own their feelings or respect the feelings of others.

Adults should help children understand the difference between assertiveness and aggression. Assertive communicators advocate for themselves while respecting the rights of others, while aggressive communicators advocate for themselves in a way that violates the rights of others. Aggressive communicators are bullies. Assertive communicators use "I" statements, maintain eye contact, and state their needs and feelings clearly and respectfully. Bullies use "you" statements, dominate conversations, and use blame and humiliation to control a situation. Help children understand the need for a balance between meeting their own needs and trying to understand and respect others' needs. Children may dislike not getting what they want all the time, but they will begin to understand why a balance is necessary.

Chapter 2

When children are allowed to believe that they deserve to get whatever they want whenever they want it, no matter who or what is in the way, they are on their way to becoming bullies. Bullying is a growing problem in child care programs, schools, families, and communities. Parents, teachers, and caregivers can address this problem by helping children understand that others may have different ideas about activities, family life, and so on. Teaching children that others' ideas are not wrong—just different—will go a long way toward helping children respect others while standing up for themselves.

The reality is that whenever people interact with other people, there are bound to be disagreements. Children practice what they see when disagreements happen among other people. If children see others pushing and shoving to get what they want, and the aggressors get the desired outcome, then the observing children store such strategies for future use. They cannot see a downside. That's why adults need to teach acceptance and respect in an intentional way.

PROVIDERS' ROLE

Intentional Teaching

Even for adults, listening is the hardest communication skill to learn. Busy adults can find it hard to be in the moment when talking with children instead of thinking of all the things they could be doing besides listening to a child. By modeling listening strategies, such as getting on children's level and making eye contact, by reading body language, by identifying feelings, and by asking questions to clarify the message being sent, adults are informally teaching communication skills while practicing them.

In addition to modeling, adults must purposefully teach the many facets of communication, from talking to listening to expressing emotions to reading body language to using digital communication wisely. Adults need to deliberately plan time and activities that allow children to practice reading body language. Create activities that encourage communication skills and help children learn to listen to others before responding. Help children learn to hear the whole conversation and then take a minute to formulate their comments. Encouraging language development and engaging children in conversation can go a long way toward improving the child's ability to communicate. Reading to children is a great way for children to hear the spoken word and appreciate the written word. Be patient when talking to children and give them time to formulate their thoughts as they begin to have two-way conversations. Effective communication skills should be taught both during an individual teachable moment and to an entire class. Help children learn to use an assertive communication style so they can provide information while still respecting others. Educate children about why aggressive communication is bullying, and why passive or passive-aggressive communication can lead to bullying. Create a no-bullying policy. If you are using digital media in your home or classroom, make sure that all media devices have content controls so that children are not viewing or participating in inappropriate online activities. Create a community where all members are special in their own way and respecting others is the norm.

Environment Design

Environmental Elements That Foster Communication

PHYSICAL ENVIRONMENT	TEMPORAL ENVIRONMENT	INTERPERSONAL ENVIRONMENT
• Child-generated list of kind and unkind words to help in developing a positive communication style	• Activities that support the identification and meaning of various body language examples	• Staff who listen to children and talk *with* children, not *at* them
• Peace table (described in chapter 5) to help children talk through problems	• Using a prop, such as a stuffed animal or a ball, to be held by the speaker to teach children that whoever holds the prop is the speaker and everyone else listens	• Staff who celebrate a diversity of opinions
• Dramatic play that allows for role-playing of familiar and unfamiliar situations	• Having a speaker's corner where children can host plays and make presentations	• Adults who encourage expression of ideas
• Journal writing and drawing to express ideas and feelings, tell stories, and practice written communication	• Role-playing to identify feelings and emotions	• Activities that encourage self-talk phrases, such as "I can do this" or "I will be all right"
• Puppets or marionettes that allow children to speak through the prop	• Scheduled time for group discussion and cooperative learning	• Adults modeling acceptable ways to deal with problems and express emotions

Environmental Elements That Foster Communication *(continued)*

PHYSICAL ENVIRONMENT	TEMPORAL ENVIRONMENT	INTERPERSONAL ENVIRONMENT
• Multiple phones for use in dramatic play	• Using pictures and words when creating and communicating rules	
• Walkie-talkies placed in different places in the room to encourage the use of words and conversation		
• Books that range in complexity from wordless to chapter books		

Strategies for Intentional Teaching and Encouraging Skill Development

- Create a feelings poster using the faces of the children in your program displaying various emotions.
- Create interactive small- and large-group activities to help children learn to listen.
- Provide journals where children can draw or write about their feelings.
- Create individual feelings charts to help children self-identify their emotions. Encourage children to change their charts when their feelings change throughout the day.
- Intentionally plan time to discuss communication skills and practice them.
- Provide a "How Would You Feel If . . ." writing center that has pictures of stressful things, like an ice-cream cone on the ground or a block tower being kicked over. Ask the children to write or draw a picture about how they would feel if these things happened to them.
- Have speakers hold a visual aid, such as a bear or ball or flower, to help children focus on and listen to the speaker.
- Get on the child's eye level when you are talking and listening to a child.
- Find ways to get children's attention when they are engrossed in play.
- Establish listening rules, such as "Only one person talks at a time."

PARENT AND STAFF EDUCATION STRATEGIES

It is never too late to learn effective communication or to improve your communication skills. As adults, we aren't always great communicators. We often listen partially to what a speaker has to say while we are formulating our shopping list, comments, ideas, or answers. Taking time to identify weaknesses within your own communication skill set and consciously changing how you communicate with other adults and children will go a long way toward helping children do the same. Communicate to staff and families through your program's parent bulletin board, emails, texts, and newsletters about the current communication skill you are working on in the classroom and how parents can support the children in the program and at home. Help families and staff understand the benefits of good communication skills. Help parents understand what bullying is and which behaviors are part of the natural process of growing up. Do your research, and post links to articles on effective communication strategies on your website or in your newsletter. Notify parents when these articles and tips are available and how to access them, or make print copies for parents who may not have access to a printer or the internet and place these copies by the parent bulletin board. Send weekly tips via text message or email about things families can do to improve their communication with children. Make sure that any communication provided to parents is in their first language whenever possible.

Even if you have been in the business of child care for years, brushing up your skills by attending a class on effective communication is always a great idea. As a child care provider, you might host a class on communication and invite both staff and parents to attend so everyone understands what you are trying to teach the children and why. Make sure that policies are in place for the use of digital communication within your program to protect the privacy and safety of the children. When you notice that a child has made positive strides in communication skills, tell the child's family and celebrate the success. The more you communicate to staff and families about what you are doing and offer tips about how to support this teaching at home, the more successful children will be at honing their communication skills.

Things to Remember

- Communication is a two-way street of both speaking and listening.
- Children need support to develop appropriate communication skills.
- Listening is the hardest communication skill to develop.
- Body language can reveal a lot about the feelings of both the speaker and the listener.
- Assertive communication is the most balanced type of communication.
- An aggressive communication style can be considered bullying.
- Identify your own communication style.
- Provide policies and controls for electronic devices used in your program.
- Intentionally designed environments play a critical part in encouraging children's communication skills.
- Children practice what they see.
- Celebrate diverse opinions.
- Encourage expression of ideas.
- Communicate with parents face-to-face and in a variety of written formats, including emails, texts, and via social media.

Children's Books Dealing with Communication

- *Big Bad Bruce* by Bill Peet
- *Can You Tell How Someone Feels?* by Nita Everly
- *Hats!* by Kevin Luthardt
- *Howard B. Wigglebottom Learns to Listen* by Howard Binkow
- *Hugo and the Bullyfrogs* by Francesca Simon
- *Interrupting Chicken* by David Ezra Stein
- *The Listening Walk* by Paul Showers
- *My Mouth Is a Volcano!* by Julia Cook
- *Understand and Care* by Cheri J. Meiners
- *A Weekend with Wendell* by Kevin Henkes
- *When I Care about Others* by Cornelia Maude Spelman
- *Words Are Not for Hurting* by Elizabeth Verdick

CHAPTER 3

Coping

WHAT IS COPING?

Coping is the ability to intentionally implement strategies to reduce stress. People need coping skills to manage the interactions of any given day effectively. Children are on the move throughout the day, in multiple places while interacting with a variety of individuals who have varying rules and expectations. For example, a child may leave home and go directly to child care, then in the middle of the day be picked up by Grandma, who will take the child to a doctor appointment. After that, they grab lunch at a nearby restaurant, then go to the playground to play. Grandma then drops the child off at home to have dinner with Mom and Dad and brother before going to the brother's sporting event. Then it's back home for bedtime. This is a lot of environments in one day. Some environments will provide successes and others will provide challenges. However, all can and do create stress for some children.

Stress in the lives of children can get in the way of their ability to control their behavior. Teaching children how to cope with stress can eliminate negative behaviors such as tantrums, hitting, and biting. Children learn how to cope with stressful situations by observing other children and adults. Adults who can control their emotions and their responses to stressful situations offer children examples of how they can do the same.

Encourage parents to give you information about events and situations that cause their children stress. Likewise, share with parents things that have happened in your care that might have caused stress for their children. This type of information sharing can help both parents and staff proactively create activities to support children going through stress. Knowing what strategies children use to de-stress at home is important, so that those same strategies can be used within a care program to create consistent support for children. (See chapter 7 for de-stressing ideas and activities.)

Each child responds differently to a particular environment. The stressors within a given environment can be different for each child. Children may find an environment too loud or too quiet. They might not like the activities provided or may not know what to do. They may not like their peers who are present. They might not like the staff, feeling staff are not fair. When you notice that a child could be stressed, the first step is to stop what you are doing and breathe. Go to the child, calling the child by name. Once there, try to determine the child's emotion by saying, "It looks like you are feeling _____," or, "You seemed _____ when you were _____." These types of statements help you make sure you are reading the situation correctly. Remove the child from where the stress-causing event took place, going to a quiet place if possible. If you or the child needs to calm down, sit quietly and say to the child, "I think we need to calm down before we can talk about what happened." You may need to help by touching the child's shoulder, holding hands, or sitting next to each other. When you are both calm, ask the child what happened. Remember that you may not have seen everything that happened—especially what took place prior to the stressful event. Usually, there is a story before the story. Give the child time to tell the whole story without rushing. The event and the feelings around it can be very intense and personal to the child, so create a sense of safety and allow the child to talk without interruption. Make sure everyone involved gets an opportunity to talk. Help children develop empathy by identifying other children's feelings and connecting them to their own feelings in similar situations. Use open-ended questions to clarify that you have understood what the child said and how the child felt.

Once you have identified the problem, then the real work begins. Help children identify appropriate ways to cope with their feelings. If children get stuck trying to come up with strategies, offer them prompts, such as "What do you think would have happened if you came to an adult?" Refrain from providing children with all the answers. Instead, engage them in identifying their emotions and encourage them to generate their own solutions to the problems they are facing. Accepting responsibility and ownership for their feelings and behaviors is the key to control and coping. So to recap, here is the basic process for helping a child cope with a stressful event:

1. Calm down (both adult and child).
2. Connect.
3. Create safety.
4. Identify feelings.

5. Display empathy.

6. Double-check information.

7. Problem solve.

It is easy to get frustrated when a child is stressed out and coping inappropriately, especially if this happens a lot. You may think, "Here we go again." If this is a regular occurrence, that's a clue that the child is missing key social skills, such as an inability to self-calm, communicate effectively, or problem solve. Refer to the observation tool in appendix A for help identifying missing skills. Once you've identified missing skills, plan lessons to help the child acquire those skills. When stressful events occur, relaxing techniques, such as slow breathing, exercise, and yoga, provide children with additional strategies to deal with stress. Until the child is calm and the story is told, the child cannot move forward toward a solution. Also, you can help reduce stress and crabbiness by providing a regular schedule, a balanced diet, consistent sleep times, consistent rules, and clear expectations.

ASSOCIATED SKILLS

Dealing with Nonsuccess

All children want to be successful. But throughout their lives, however hard they try, they will sometimes struggle. When children feel they are failing, their confidence lags, and they begin to believe that they are not capable. This is when you hear "I can't do it," or "You do it for me." Once children believe they are not capable, this belief becomes a self-fulfilling prophecy.

So how do we reverse this downward spiral and make children feel capable of trying new things? Children take their cues from adults. If you are always trying to make artwork perfect or the snack area spotless, or are always doing things for children that they can do for themselves, you are sending the message that you don't believe children are capable of completing tasks correctly. You do this without uttering a single word. It is often your actions or those of other children that define children's strengths and incapabilities. A message of incapability, even in small things, can create problems for a child's self-confidence.

Some children have a fearful temperament. They will lag behind and watch a game or an activity to see how others do things before entering the activity.

For example, preschool children may stand on the outside of the sensory area and watch because they have never seen a sensory table before or because they do not like to get messy. You may need to provide these children with a smock or stand by them while they experiment at the sensory table. You can also create nontraditional participation options for preschoolers, such as picture maker or storyteller. As children get older and play games together or participate in sports, some may be reluctant to participate because they've never played the game before and don't know the rules, so they feel inadequate. You can offer these children ways to participate on the sidelines, such as being a line judge, scorekeeper, or cheerleader. Not all children like all activities that are offered within a program, so an array of activities and games that span a wide range of interests and abilities will help children achieve success and develop confidence. Adults need to be classroom cheerleaders, not participation dictators. When you see a child trying something new, give genuine positive feedback, such as "You really worked hard on that picture," or "Wow, look how many more blocks you used in this tower!" These small comments validate children's successes.

Designing the space so children can play side by side or in small groups helps create peer teaching opportunities. Children can help one another by teaching how to play a game, showing how they drew a flower, demonstrating how to dribble a basketball, or being a reading mentor. Often children want to help others and can be more patient than adults. Peer teaching can help children learn skills with the benefit of other children's perspectives. Peer teaching is a win-win approach because it gives the learning child information at their level and it gives the teaching child opportunities to cement their own success as they teach another child. Sometimes an adult may need to guide a child in need to another child with the needed skill because the child in need doesn't know whom to ask for help. In addition, staff should take note of skills children want to master and plan activities to support that growth. Intentionally designing the physical environment to include quiet places to regroup and calm down is beneficial to children who struggle to cope with nonsuccess. This combination of purposefully designing the environment to support the mastery of a skill, peer teaching, sideline participation, and verbal and nonverbal support can help children become successful.

Dealing with a Crisis

A crisis is an event that happens with little or no warning that negatively affects the security of an individual or group of individuals. Some examples of crises are environmental disasters (fire, tornado, flood, or hurricane), mass shootings, family illness, death, unemployment, moving to a new house, drug use, foster care, the loss of a pet, or the addition of a new family member, such as a stepparent or baby. A crisis that seems insignificant to adults can be a major event to a child because it is an unexpected disruption of the norm.

Crises happen in the lives of all children and adults. Sometimes crises seem to be happening constantly. It is how people respond to a crisis that is important. According to the National Association of School Psychologists (NASP), "Recognizing a child's individual coping style enables parents, teachers and other caregivers to better support their needs and reinforce their coping strengths" (2015). Different children may react to similar situations in different ways. Even siblings can act totally different when faced with the same crisis. For example, one sibling might be excited to have a new baby in the family, but another sibling may be upset about having to share their parents' attention. Children react to crises in many ways. Some become withdrawn and lose interest in friends or school. Others begin to act younger, using baby talk or sucking their thumbs. Still others may act out, not understanding why the crisis has happened and not knowing what to do with the emotions they are feeling. Some children become more afraid of the dark or of being left alone. Children may complain of stomachaches and headaches. These are all normal reactions to a crisis, so adults need to be understanding toward these behaviors and respond in a calm way. Children in crisis look to adults to know how to feel and what to do. During any crisis, large or small, a child needs reassurance, words of encouragement, and empathy.

Jenny was five years old. She had been in the same early childhood program since she was an infant. She was a carefree child, well liked by her peers and the staff. Shortly after she turned five, Jenny came to class and was extremely moody. All day she was out of sorts and picking fights with her peers. The staff mentioned to Jenny's mother at pickup that they thought Jenny might be coming down with something and described Jenny's behavior throughout the day. Jenny's mother said she would watch her over the weekend to make sure she was OK to return on Monday.

After a few days, Jenny's behavior had not improved. The staff asked her mother if something had happened recently that might have upset Jenny. Her mother confided that the family was going through a rough time. Jenny's dad had been laid off, and they were barely able to make the rent. In addition, Jenny's grandmother was having health problems that limited her time with Jenny. Jenny's mother said that Jenny and her grandmother usually spent every Sunday together, and that hadn't happened for three Sundays in a row. Jenny's mom asked, "Do you think she is acting out because of all this?"

The staff worked with the parents to find community resources for heat, food, and rent assistance. The staff explained to the parent that it was important for Jenny to be able to talk about how she was feeling and that this might take some time. The staff discussed ways to help Jenny deal with the stress of missing her grandmother.

Children's lives are controlled by adults. As adults deal with their own stress, children feed off of the emotions of adults in their lives. If the adults are worried, so are children. In the scenario about Jenny, her world had been turned upside down. When things were rough at home, usually she could spend time with her grandmother, and then Jenny would feel that everything was OK. But when her grandmother got sick, Jenny felt lost.

When children are upset, their feelings are all mixed up. It took a long time for Jenny to express that she felt scared and alone. She had so many questions. She needed an adult to talk to who was patient enough to wait for her to talk.

Together the staff and Jenny's mother came up with strategies to help Jenny deal with the separation from her grandmother. The staff requested a picture of Jenny's grandmother and placed it in her cubby so she could see her grandmother's face whenever she wanted. Jenny's mother scheduled time for Jenny to talk to her grandmother daily, and after a few weeks Jenny got to visit her. The staff helped Jenny create cards for her grandmother in the art area and mail the cards to her. Each of these strategies allowed Jenny to feel in control and connected to her grandmother.

So how can adults minimize the effects of crises in children's lives? First and foremost, caregivers need to realize that they cannot eliminate crises, because children spend limited time in school and child care. However, teachers and caregivers can play an important role in how children face a crisis and manage their feelings.

If the crisis is a community crisis, protect children from the outside world by limiting media exposure. Although adults may need to hear the latest report on a community crisis, children do not. They are not able to process the information presented on news programs. News media may provide reports and images that are too graphic for children. Repeated exposure to photos, videos, and stories about neighborhood shootings, robberies, or assaults—or events such as accidents, natural disasters, or war—can cause children to become desensitized to violence. It can also lead children to suppress trauma instead of dealing with it. Or they may become more confused and upset at what is shown and still unable to understand its implications.

During any crisis, the children involved are the most vulnerable and the least able to correct the situation. Create a sense of safety for children in crisis by providing comfort items such as a blanket, a favorite toy, or pictures of family members. Provide more one-on-one time with the child if needed or requested, and encourage parents to spend more time together as a family. Meet with parents to determine what the family has told the child about the crisis, and follow their lead. Encourage parents to give truthful answers to the child's questions and provide basic facts. Reiterate that the child's safety is your top priority. Listen to the child without judgment and without minimizing their fears and concerns. It takes time for children to formulate ideas and express feelings. If you get confused when talking to a child about a crisis, ask open-ended questions to make sure you understand. Make sure you repeat often that adults are doing everything possible to keep the child safe. When children do not want to talk, encourage them to use art and journal writing as an avenue for expressing their feelings in another way. This strategy can provide you with information and an opportunity to validate children's fears and feelings. Encourage free play, which is a natural de-stresser that can help children release bottled-up energy. Play can also offer children an opportunity to act out what happened and how they feel about the event.

Once again, adults need to model coping skills. Such modeling helps children know how to act and can also help adults manage their own feelings. First, some private time will help you make sense of what has happened and how you are going to respond to the children. If you calmly acknowledge that you are sad now, but that you also know things will be better soon, you show children that it is OK to be sad when something bad has happened and that you will work together to make it better. Getting back to a normal routine of sleeping, eating, playing with friends, and returning to school and child care as soon as possible will help children feel safe. Creating a two-way communication system between family members and teachers is important. This two-way communication helps adults share information and provide appropriate support and comfort. It also allows you to modify supports in a timely manner when needed.

Anger Management

Having a wide array of feelings is part of human nature. Sometimes feelings can be very strong. Anger is a strong feeling that can be overwhelming, but anger itself is not bad. It is not the anger, but rather how people sometimes act when they are angry, that can be problematic. How people act on their feelings is a choice. In the heat of an angry moment, people sometimes strike out at others. Then, rather than take responsibility for what they've done, people tend to blame others for making them feel angry. Following are some situations that often trigger anger in children:

- having something taken from them
- not getting something they want
- being physically harmed (kicked, hit, tripped, shoved, and so on)
- being spoken to hurtfully
- being made to do something they do not want to do
- being excluded or rejected by peers
- feeling that no one cares
- separation from family members
- not being in a safe place

Different children have different triggers, so adults need to be aware of what might trigger anger in a specific child. When adults are aware of these triggers, they can help children separate their feelings from their actions. Once children understand that they are angry, the next step for adults is to teach the children to cool down and refocus on solving the problem that made them angry.

Anger can manifest itself in a flash. Sometimes children get so tied up in their anger that they forget why they got angry in the first place. It is easy to take children's anger to heart. But as an adult caregiver, you should resist being offended or upset by children's anger. Your role is to help children take responsibility for any inappropriate behavior they've displayed in anger. Help children understand that they've made a mistake, but this mistake is over, and the only thing they can do about it is what they do next. Remember that just because children are angry, that does not necessarily mean that they are angry at you. Before you talk to an angry child, calm yourself so you can focus on the child to determine the source of the problem. Sometimes deep breathing helps calm both the adult and the child. Calming occurs when you breathe out longer than you breathe in. Taking time in a quiet area away from the group is another way to help yourself and an angry child calm down and get ready for a conversation. Once all involved parties are calm, the conversation can begin.

Finding out what caused a child's anger is like peeling an onion layer by layer to see what is in the center. The first thing you see is the behavior. But the behavior is a result of an emotion that a child is having a hard time containing or communicating. Help the child identify the emotion. For example, you might say, "You must be really angry to _____ [describe the behavior]. Is that correct?" This statement tells the child which action made you suspect anger. It also shows that you understand the child is upset. This strategy can prevent the child from escalating. Let the child tell his or her story without interruption. Once the child has finished, use open-ended questions to clarify what you hear. This will help you better understand what caused the child's strong emotion.

Once you understand what caused the behavior, you can help the child identify other strategies that might have helped achieve the desired result in more appropriate ways. Begin by asking if the behavior got the child what he or she wanted. Then follow up by asking what else the child could have done to change the outcome. Help the child create a list of other options. For a preschooler, collecting pictures that will help the child remember what to do when anger surfaces again may be useful. Encourage a school-age child to write down suggested alternatives to create a tool the child can use later. This process might feel time-consuming at first, but with regular use, the adult will be able to walk through the steps quickly, and the child will soon learn other strategies to use when strong emotions bubble up.

Self-Control

The group of skills children need to control their emotions, thoughts, and actions is called *executive function*. Executive function comprises three skills: self-control, working memory, and mental flexibility. *Working memory* is the ability to remember and use pieces of information for a short period of time. *Mental flexibility* is the ability to maintain or change attention as different demands occur, or to apply different rules in different environments. People who do not have self-control do things without thinking about the consequences. When a person who does have self-control encounters a difficult situation and a strong emotion surfaces, self-control allows the person to delay action and think about the options available to manage the emotion.

For young children, controlling their own emotions, thoughts, and actions is a difficult task. Self-control skills are managed by a part of the brain called the prefrontal cortex. The prefrontal cortex does not develop fully until age twenty-five. According to researchers at Harvard University's Center on the Developing Child (2017), children are born not with self-control, but rather with the potential to develop this skill. Adults need to help children develop it.

In 1968 a Stanford University researcher named Walter Mischel conducted an experiment to better understand self-control. In this experiment (often called the marshmallow test), a child could choose to have one treat immediately or wait several minutes and get two treats. When Mischel revisited his marshmallow-test subjects as adolescents, "he found that teenagers who had waited longer for the marshmallows as preschoolers were more likely to score higher on the SAT, and their parents were more likely to rate them as having a greater ability to plan, handle stress, respond to reason, and exhibit self-control in frustrating situations and concentrate without becoming distracted." Mischel and his colleagues followed up again when the subjects were in their forties. The researchers found, through a different adult-focused test, that the subjects' self-control skills (or lack thereof) remained consistent. Mischel and his colleagues concluded that some people are simply more sensitive to emotional triggers than others are, and that these differences persist throughout their lifetimes (APA 2018; APA 2012).

When children become angry, a fight-or-flight response often happens. The fight-or-flight response is a biological reaction that prepares our body to protect itself when we perceive danger. The heart beats rapidly, body temperature rises and the skin flushes and sweats, breathing accelerates, and muscles tense. It is important for children to recognize this response before they act on it. By observing closely, you may be able to see the physical signs of fight-or-flight in children even before they realize them. You can help children switch fight-or-flight to executive function by using calming techniques such as deep breathing. (If children can smile before they breathe, this act switches them from the emotional state to the executive state.) Go to children and intercede before they lose control. Identify what you are seeing to help children connect the body's signals to the beginning of an out-of-control anger episode. Help children understand that when their body begins to send these signals, they are becoming frustrated and angry. Have children identify the signals that they notice and talk about what they can do when they notice these signals. Once children understand and can identify their fight-or-flight signals, they can stop impulsive, angry actions before they start—or before they escalate. It is only in this state that children can find solutions.

It is important that children practice self-control strategies and games while they are calm, and not when they are in the middle of conflict or a stressful situation. So how can you help children learn to control their impulses? Begin by helping them understand the program's rules and behavior expectations so there are no misunderstandings about how they should act within the program. Every time a limit is set and children abide by that limit, they are learning self-control. When children learn to wait their turn or for lunch to be served, they are learning self-control. When children ultimately get to take a turn or eat lunch, they learn that with patience they will eventually get what they want (even though they may have felt frustrated while waiting). Traditional childhood games like Simon says, red light/green light, army/navy, colored eggs, and freeze tag require children to listen, wait, follow directions, and delay gratification. These games are fun ways to help children learn to control their natural impulses outside of conflict so this self-control can become easier within conflict.

PROVIDERS' ROLE

Intentional Teaching

To cope with stress, children need to find a way to calm themselves. Calming themselves helps children move from out-of-control behavior toward conflict resolution or effective communication. Help children learn to self-soothe with things like deep breathing, clenching their hands and relaxing them, rubbing their arms, or having someone brush their hair or rub their back. Offer children relaxing activities, such as painting, drawing, and reading, in areas with a variety of art supplies and books. These types of activities can give children an opportunity to get deep in thought and can allow them to lose themselves in work and leave their frustration behind. Work together with parents to share information about things that cause stress in children. This will help provide continuity of support from all the caregivers in children's lives. Encourage children to use journals to help them express their feelings.

Adults can help children develop coping skills by paying special attention to the environment. Create a soft area within the environment where children can relax and de-stress. Soft elements can include beanbag chairs, large floor pillows, and area rugs. A soft area provides a contrast to the typical hard chairs and cement or tile flooring of a classroom. Within this area, include a variety of prescreened music and headphones, along with stress balls and fidgets. A fidget is a small toy that can be manipulated by children or adults to reduce stress or increase concentration. You can also place feelings journals in this area and visual aids or charts showing how to calm down or deal with feelings. It is a great place to have a peace table (see chapter 5).

Children always seem to favor one area in a program, and given space constraints or available supplies, teachers need to limit the number of children using that space. To help children self-monitor spaces within your program, provide visual aids that indicate how many children can play within each space. Give each child a name tag to place on the visual aid at each space. As the spots for name tags fill up, children can clearly see whether the space has room for them to play. When children really want to play in a particular area that is full, they learn that they will have to wait sometimes. Create waiting lists for children in popular areas so children can sign up when an area has reached its occupancy limit. Here's how to make an occupancy visual aid or a waiting list for a group of children who may or may not be able to read:

1. Write each child's name on a piece of card stock. Affix the child's photo next to the name and attach an adhesive Velcro dot on the back side of the name card.
2. Use a piece of laminated card stock with three Velcro dots to serve as an occupancy list. Use another piece of laminated card stock with three Velcro dots to serve as a waiting list.

Post both lists and a basket with the name cards at the entrance to any area that needs them.

Preschoolers may need help from adults as they begin this process, but soon using the lists will become routine. When a child's name is on a waiting list, an adult should let the children who are currently playing in the space know that there is someone on the waiting list. Occupancy and waiting lists help playing children be aware of other children's needs, and they help the other children understand that sometimes they have to wait. Lists also help children understand that it is not the adult but the space that limits access to a play area. To help children learn how to delay gratification, play fun interactive games that require children to follow directions or wait before acting.

Often when children become frustrated or angry, their bodies send messages that they are becoming stressed. When children recognize these signals, they can use relaxing and re-centering strategies. To help children self-identify how they are feeling and what they can do about it, create individualized anger meters. An anger meter can show several levels of anger by using a color gradient paint chip from your local paint store. Explain to the children that the intensity of color indicates the intensity of feelings; lighter shades indicate less intense feelings, while darker shades indicate stronger feelings. Alongside each shade, indicate what to do to calm down. For children who cannot read, use both words and pictures to tell and show what children can do to calm down. For instance, the word *breathing* can be accompanied by a picture of a child doing deep breathing, the phrase *clenching fist* can be paired with a picture of a child's fist, and so on. Each child might have different triggers and different soothing strategies. Observation can give adults clues that indicate when a child is close to a meltdown or when a child is attempting to maintain or regain control. By keeping track of children who have limited coping skills and documenting new stressors or management skills when these are identified for each child, adults can be proactive when children are in crisis.

Environment Design

Environmental Elements That Foster Coping

PHYSICAL ENVIRONMENT	TEMPORAL ENVIRONMENT	INTERPERSONAL ENVIRONMENT
• Quiet space where children can regroup and relax, equipped with soft elements, such as pillows and upholstered furniture	• Consistent schedules in all program spaces	• Providing one-on-one time with staff to share emotions
• Book area with soft furniture and beanbag chairs for relaxation	• Advance notice of schedule changes	• Identifying activities that have a calming effect on children and integrating them in the program
• Music area with a variety of prescreened music	• Time to teach and practice calming strategies when children are not in crisis mode	• Providing places for children to store comfort items
• Independent play activities such as puzzles, creative art, and journal writing		• Encouraging children to bring pictures of family members

Strategies for Intentional Teaching and Encouraging Skill Development

Following is a list of just a few activities you can plan to encourage the social skills involved in coping. (Many activities can foster coping skills, so this is not an exhaustive list.)

- Include children in setting rules so they know and understand the behavior expectations in your program.
- Help children take responsibility for their actions.
- Provide activities that help children de-stress and relax.
- Create opportunities for children to practice self-control.
- Provide activities and program spaces to help children learn how to react appropriately to stress, crises, and anger.
- Engage in conversation and direct teaching to help children understand their stressors and those of others.
- Teach children ways to de-stress and think before they speak.

PARENT AND STAFF EDUCATION STRATEGIES

Explaining coping skills to parents and family members is important. While parents and staff may understand that a child is stressed or not acting normally, they may not understand the coping skills that the child is missing. As children deal with stress, sometimes adults feel that the children are being too sensitive and need to get over it. Often adults react with frustration rather than compassion. Defining the many aspects of stress and the skills needed to cope with stress can help parents and staff understand why children act a certain way. Typically, if a child is stressed, so are the child's family members. When you are designing activities and strategies to help children deal with stress, share them with parents and families so they can integrate these strategies at home. Find community resources for dealing with a variety of crises that affect families and children, such as heat assistance, grief counseling, health clinics, food banks, and disaster relief. Find these resources proactively, before they are needed. Use your parent bulletin board and other communication systems to make parents and families aware of coping strategies that your program is using and what the benefits of these strategies are. Helping parents and families learn how to deal with stress will ultimately help children learn to manage their own stress.

Things to Remember

As you plan for children who do not have positive coping skills, look to the environment and eliminate as many stressors as possible. Maximize children's success through intentionally teaching coping skills and providing activities to support ongoing development of these skills. Here are a few strategies that may help children learn coping skills:

- Create opportunities for children to de-stress as they learn yoga, participate in an exercise group, or relax in the book area.
- Teach children to breathe deeply when they feel stressed.
- Create spaces where children can unwind, such as a corner with a few large pillows on the floor where children can listen to prescreened music.
- Allow children to have comfort items to use when life gets overwhelming.

- Provide a place for children to display pictures of their families.
- Outdoors, put a blanket under a tree so children can just relax.
- Provide an indoor space where children can gather and chat with friends.
- Provide a quiet place equipped with posters that outline strategies for regaining emotional control when children feel overwhelmed.
- Provide children with expressive, engaging activities, such as photography or painting.

Children's Books Dealing with Coping Skills

- *The Fall of Freddie the Leaf* by Leo Buscaglia
- *Goodbye, Mousie* by Robie H. Harris
- *I Miss You* by Pat Thomas
- *The Little Bully* by Beth Bracken
- *Llama Llama and the Bully Goat* by Anna Dewdney
- *The Next Place* by Warren Hanson
- *Saying Goodbye to Lulu* by Corinne Demas
- *Stand Tall, Molly Lou Melon* by Patty Lovell
- *Thinking of Mom* by M. O. Lufkin
- *When My Worries Get Too Big!* by Kari Dunn Buron

CHAPTER 4

Community Building

WHAT IS COMMUNITY BUILDING?

A community is a group of people with varied characteristics joined by location and common goals. In a community, individuals should feel safe, and each person should have a role within the group. A community can be found within a child care facility, child care home, school, or family home. A community develops when the children feel valued, understand their role within the program or home, and develop a feeling of ownership.

A community can be built in any space where adults care for children. Every individual should play a role in building the community and creating its success. This means that each person takes responsibility for their own actions and participates in maintaining the community. The community as a whole needs to support its individual members by encouraging independence, helping them feel competent and valued, and keeping them safe. Helping children become responsible, independent, and competent begins with not doing for children what they can do for themselves. For example, if children take toys out, then they can put the toys away. Children can put their trash in the garbage or clear their dishes after lunch.

As community members, children have a responsibility to maintain the community by doing age-appropriate chores. Children like and need to have jobs. When you are assigning jobs to children, start with small, easily completed jobs, such as hanging up their coats, setting the table at mealtime, or putting toys away after free-choice time. Then move to more difficult tasks, like washing dishes, clearing their dishes after lunch, or washing the snack table off when snack is over. Rotate jobs so all children have an opportunity to do each job. Jobs such as a line leader, door holder, art assistant, and snack assistant help young children feel important and valued.

It is essential to tell children what is expected with each job. While door holder and line leader are easy to understand just by name, other jobs, such as snack assistant and art assistant, may need to be explained. The job duties may change based on the ages and abilities of children. For instance, a snack assistant in a preschool classroom may pass out the drinks, napkins, and snacks at snacktime. A snack assistant in a school-age room might count out the needed snacks, napkins, and cups, then place them in the snack area and put leftovers away when snacktime has ended. With guidance and clearly expressed expectations, children can complete jobs successfully.

Children may not complete a job perfectly at first. What you think is correct may not be what they think is correct. Mastery takes practice, so allow children to practice. If needed, do the job with them the first few times, then encourage them to do it on their own—or post a picture of how you would like the completed task to look so children know what you expect. Remind children that you are not expecting perfection, but rather completion. Once children know that they can make positive contributions to the community, they will learn to take responsibility for those contributions, develop a sense of ownership, and feel pride in a job well done. With each job you assign children, you send the message that they are capable and instill confidence.

When children take part in developing community rules, they seldom argue about those rules, because people seldom argue with their own data. Including children in rule development helps them feel that they have some control over their environment. Allowing input helps children feel valued, creates a sense of confidence, and develops empathy and an understanding of the needs of their peers. When adults take a "my way or the highway" attitude when setting rules, this limits the children's ability to participate in community building and diminishes their sense of ownership. If rules are developed without the children's input, this may limit children's buy in to the classroom community. Including children in the rulemaking process helps them understand why rules are made and how rules keep them safe.

When you are developing community rules together, talk about safety first and then kindness. Ask, "What rules do we need to make everyone safe?" Then ask, "What rules do we need to make this a kind place?" Refrain from using words like *stop*, *no*, *don't*, and *quit*, because rules stated as prohibitions, or what *not* to do, assume that children know what you want them to do. That can be a dangerous assumption. When you are writing the rules, choose words that tell the children what you want them to do, such as "Use quiet voices. Use kind words. Use walking feet. Make safe choices." You will need to help children understand what kind words and safe choices are by asking questions and charting their answers. This activity will give you an idea of what children think these words mean. Once you have discussed the rules with children, place your discussion chart next to the rules so both can be reviewed as needed. When your community is generating rules, you should also generate consequences. Children often come up with far harsher consequences than adults do. You may need to adjust consequences to accommodate the children's age and development.

How the environment is designed plays a large role in building the community. A safe, nonjudgmental community environment allows children to try new roles, practice social skills, investigate new areas of interest, and use trial and error to make sense of the world around them. The environment needs to be equipped with materials and activities that allow for skill building while still presenting a challenge. Just as children need to participate in rulemaking, they also need a voice in designing their physical space. When a space for children is designed with their input, it becomes a place they enjoy and want to preserve. Program spaces are as varied as the types of programs, ages and numbers of children attending, and locations of programs. Regardless of these variables, providing a variety of spaces and activities to meet the needs of all the children is important. When you are looking at new themes for lesson plans, you can increase children's engagement by asking them what types of activities and centers they would like. Make sure there are enough age-appropriate materials within the centers and adequate supplies for the number of children allowed in each center. This approach can minimize negative behaviors that surface when children cannot find activities they are interested in or when there are not enough materials and supplies for children to play with.

ASSOCIATED SKILLS

Friendship Skills

The old saying "No man is an island" is so true. Humans need others around them. To thrive people need not only their families but also their acquaintances and friends.

Like adults, children have both acquaintances and friends. An acquaintance is a person whom one knows but who is not a close friend. A friend is one person attached to another by affection or esteem. Helping children define the word *friend* is an important step toward understanding what they need to do to be a friend. Encourage children to generate definitions, and post them to help children remember. The next step is to help children explain why friends are good to have and identify fun things to do with friends. Again, chart and post these child-generated ideas. They can serve as reminders when things are not so friendly. This should not be a one-time activity. It should be repeated and reviewed regularly, because children forget why it is important to be a friend and have a friend until they want someone to play with.

Friendships play an important role in the lives of children. According to developmental psychologists Anita Gurian and Alice Pope (2009), "Starting young and continuing through adulthood, friendships are among the most important activities of life." Friendship provides opportunities to have fun, share personal secrets, defuse stress, and problem solve. Through friendship, children can learn that all people are equal and that friends advocate for and support one another. Friends may buffer children and adolescents from negative life events, such as family conflict, illness, homelessness, and unemployment. Friendships help develop cooperation skills and provide companionship.

Children need friendship skills to both make and keep friends. Temperament can affect children's ability to learn friendship skills. (See the chart of temperament characteristics in chapter 1 on page 10.) Children with a flexible temperament typically find it easier to make and keep friends than do children with a feisty or fearful temperament.

Toddlers' and preschoolers' friendships typically develop based on physical proximity. Toddlers and preschoolers may become friends when their families live in the same neighborhood or attend the same child care program, playgroup, place of worship, and so on. They may also have similar likes and dislikes, common interests, and shared rules. Some of these friendships last, but most are short-lived. Toddlers and preschoolers can identify who their friends are, but those friendships vacillate.

In Ms. Kari's classroom of twelve preschoolers, the children were engaged in free play prior to lunch. In the dramatic play area, three girls were playing house. Stacie was the mom, Cindy was the baby, and Gianna was the dad. The children had been playing for a few minutes when a ruckus started. As Ms. Kari moved toward the group, she heard the following exchange.

Gianna said, "But can't I be the baby now? I don't want to be the dad anymore!"

Stacie said, "If you don't want to be the dad, then we don't need you to play with us."

Cindy said, "You are not my friend anymore."

Gianna stomped off and said, "You're not my friend either."

The staff watched as Gianna moved to the art area and began to create a collage with flower pictures. After five minutes of playing in the dramatic play space without Gianna as the dad, Cindy and Stacie left the space and went straight for the art area. Ms. Kari moved closer to the art area to see if Cindy and Stacie could play with Gianna again without incident.

Cindy and Stacie sat at the same table as Gianna. They asked Gianna what she was making, and with a smile Gianna explained. It wasn't long before the three girls were sitting side by side talking and laughing together.

Ms. Kari moved close to the girls to monitor the conflict, but she did not ntervene. Instead, she waited to see how the conflict would play out. Gianna was adamant that she was done playing the dad and seemed to feel OK about leaving the group. It would have been easy for Ms. Kari to focus on the comment "You are not my friend" and jump in and impose a solution that nobody wanted. But Ms. Kari understood that off-and-on friendships are a way for young children to practice friendship skills, such as collaboration, negotiation, and empathy.

Young schoolagers—especially those just starting school, a new before- or after-school child care program, or extracurricular activities—may find themselves in an unfamiliar place with faces they don't recognize. Often they are immersed rather suddenly in a structured world with rigid schedules and little free time. In potentially stressful situations like this, children need friends for shelter in the storm. Let's take a look at the following story.

Mr. Small had a large group of kindergarteners one year. The children came from a variety of places, and most had not attended preschool. Sara and Melanie met on the first day of kindergarten. They seemed to be meant for each other. They liked many of the same things and even had the same backpack. During outdoor time or free-choice time, they played together.

Sara had some health issues that made it difficult for her to control her behavior. She often blurted out words or just got up and walked around in the middle of class. Because of her health issues and her lack of experience attending school, Sara was confused about the classroom expectations.

Melanie had many friends, but she never excluded Sara. Melanie introduced Sara to other children and explained what Sara liked and did not like. Melanie seemed to be able to help Sara calm down and avoid a meltdown. She often helped other children understand what Sara needed in order to play with them.

Mr. Small quickly noticed the calming effect that Melanie had on Sara. He moved Melanie to Sara's table. When Sara left her seat, Melanie put her arm around Sara and led her back to her seat. While Melanie was understanding about Sara's needs, she still held Sara accountable.

During free-choice time, Melanie and Sara were sitting side by side playing in the puzzle area. Mr. Small said, "It is time to clean up and get ready for lunch."

Sara got up and walked away. Mr. Small moved near the puzzle area and listened, to be available if a meltdown occurred.

Melanie called Sara back and said, "Hey, Sara, you need to help put away the puzzles, because you were playing with me."

Sara said, "I'm hungry. Let's go to lunch."

Melanie said, "I will get in line after we put the puzzle away. That is the rule."

Sara walked back to the puzzle area and began handing Melanie puzzle pieces that were on the floor. Working together, they put the puzzles away, then went and washed their hands for lunch.

Sara and Melanie's friendship was built on mutual interests and acceptance of Sara's limitations. Melanie included all the children in her play, but she was particularly sensitive to Sara's needs. When push came to shove, Melanie held Sara accountable and seemed to know how to do this without upsetting Sara. Mr. Small could have stepped in and showed Melanie and Sara who was the boss of the classroom, but instead he allowed Melanie to gently redirect Sara and stood ready to help out if Sara had a meltdown.

When children enter elementary school, friendships become less adult-organized than they were in preschool. School-age children meet their peers in the classroom, at lunch, and during recess. Parents can't choose who is in any of the school groupings. This leaves the children to determine whom they want to play with. They tend to gravitate toward classmates who share their interests. Older children may also seek friends who are loyal and trustworthy, with whom they can discuss private feelings without fear of disclosure to others. School-age children can label their feelings, so unlike toddlers and pre-schoolers, they are less likely to throw a tantrum, cry, or hit when distressed.

Emma and Krista were sitting in the after-school program's homework center. Krista asked Emma, "What's up? You seem sad."

Emma said, "I just cannot get this math. It's dumb."

Krista asked, "Did you talk to Mr. Pickett about it?"

Emma shrugged and said, "Yes, but it didn't help. I don't know what to do. My parents are going to be mad if I get a bad grade."

Krista responded, "My mom went crazy about my science grade. She could not understand that I just didn't get it."

Emma asked, "So what did you do?"

Krista smiled and said, "I begged my big brother for help. He is a jerk sometimes, but he was good at explaining science. Emma, do you want me to look at this and see if I can help?"

Emma said, "Sure! Thanks, Krista!"

School-age children have the ability to show empathy, as they can relate to a friend's experience by recalling their own similar experience. Krista tried to label what she was seeing in Emma's body language by asking if she was sad. She gave Emma time to tell her story. Krista validated Emma's feelings by telling her own personal story. That helped Emma understand that Krista really knew how she felt.

During elementary school, friendship groups typically comprise children of the same gender. Both boys and girls desire friendships. They are looking for emotional support, secret keeping, and peers with similar interests. During the elementary years, children begin to compare themselves with others. These social comparisons can help children clearly define their own identities. Take time to create activities that help children reflect on what a friend should be and how to make friends. Such activities can be helpful resources for children when they are having trouble making or keeping friends. Following are some questions you might use to help children think through friendship:

- What is a friend?
- What makes a good friend?
- How can you introduce yourself to someone?
- What are some kind words?
- How do you ask someone to play?
- Why are friends good to have?
- How can we find out what others like to do?
- What are the names of your current friends?

Using a flip chart, record the responses to the above questions and place the chart in an area children visit often. It can serve as a reminder to the staff as well as the children. This activity is best suited to schoolagers, but you could modify it for preschoolers. Most preschoolers cannot read the words on the chart, but it is important that they take part in a conversation like this. Include picture cues for nonreaders to help these children remember the traits of a good friend. This should not be a one-time activity; reinforce it during group time and individual conversations.

In addition, for private reflection or individual work, use journals for children to write or draw pictures about what a good friend is or who their friends are. (For children who cannot write, adults should write as children describe their pictures.) Writing center prompts in the writing area can help children think about the many aspects of friendships. Provide three-by-five cards so children can make a booklet that includes some friend-making tips for future reference. (For children who cannot write, use pictures to convey strategies.) As children add strategies to these cards, they provide a helpful handbook that children can refer to when they want to make a friend or when they are having difficulty entering a playgroup. As the conversation continues, children can add more cards or journal entries based on additional questions about reading body language, being a good sport, dealing with anger, communicating, and so on.

Children can learn the skills needed to establish friendships long before a play situation arises. Help children develop friendships by intentionally teaching the following six strategies:

- greeting other children
- finding similar interests
- avoiding bragging
- asking interesting questions
- giving honest compliments
- doing acts of kindness

Children like to be noticed, valued, cared for, and respected. When you call children by their given name, they feel all these things. Endearments such as *sweetie*, *honey*, and *buddy*, while well-meaning, may have alternate meanings to a child and should be avoided. Encourage children and adults to acknowledge others as they enter into the program space by saying, "Hi, _____, I'm glad you are here today." This type of acknowledgment shows children how to greet others in a polite and friendly way. As an adult in the program, remember that you are a role model. How you talk to others is the example that children will follow. If you ignore children and speak to them only when they are in trouble, children will notice that. Children believe that people care about them when they are paying attention to them. Children crave attention. Negative or positive attention is equally desirable; it is the adult connection that children crave. If children feel the only way that adults notice them is through negative behavior, then negative behaviors may be all you see. Most often children will be what you believe them to be. If children think adults believe they are "bad," then they will act badly. If children think adults believe they are "good," then they will strive to be good. Similarly, if children and adults formulate a negative opinion about children that they are not good friends, this will further alienate them from their peer group.

Often children know what they like to do but cannot find others who like to do the same things. Adults may have to pair up children with similar interests. Sometimes it is easy to see what children are interested in by just looking at their backpack or clothes or what they bring in to share. However, that strategy is not always foolproof, so adults should take a little time to ask children about what they like, as in the following scenario.

In a class of four-year-olds, a child named Braxton had chronic difficulty finding a playmate. Braxton was not prone to behavior problems. However, he was a bit of a loner and had a fearful temperament. He entered the program in midyear, when the children already had their social groups established, and he just didn't seem to fit in.

During circle time, the teacher introduced graphs as a math concept. The teacher said, "In order to make the graph, we need to compare things, and today we will be using things we like." She'd already had a conversation with Braxton about what he liked, so she knew he liked dinosaurs. She weaved dinosaurs into the activity. She wrote a variety of known interests, including dinosaurs, on sentence strips and taped them to the floor. She polled the children about their interests. She had the children stand in lines in front of their interest strips. (Children could opt out if none of the interest areas appealed to them.) Once the children had formed a human graph, the teacher encouraged the children to talk to those in their line about why they liked that interest, and what they liked most about it. The teacher then posted a blank, labeled graph on the wall. Taking turns, the children each colored in a square on the posted graph to represent themselves.

The conversations among the children were interesting. They ranged from a few words to a detailed explanation. Braxton discovered that there were other students in his class who liked dinosaurs. He talked on and on about which dinosaur toys, figures, books, and movies he had. The other children could not get a word in edgewise.

The teacher followed up by asking, "So what do these graphs tell us about our classmates?"

One child said, "We all like stuff."

"That is true," said the teacher, "but what else?"

Braxton said, "That Todd and Rashawn like dinosaurs—just like me!"

"That's right," said the teacher, "so now many of us know who likes the same things we do. This afternoon during free-choice time, you will know who likes to play the same things as you do, so if you need someone to play with, you can choose someone you have never played with before." That afternoon, playgroup dynamics changed, and Braxton was invited to play.

The teacher used this simple math activity not only to teach the children about graphs, but also to inform all the children about the interests of their classmates. As a result, the children looked to others with similar interests as playmates during free-choice time. In addition, the teacher used information from the math activity to create interest areas that mirrored those discussed by the children. Not only did the children in the playgroups change, but the environments' interest areas also changed, creating a responsive environment meeting the needs of all the children.

For young children, bragging about things they have done and what they have accomplished is natural. It's like a sales pitch, saying, "Pick me, pick me!" To make a friend, a child needs to be a friend. For a child in the "I-me" period of life, however, it is a stretch to think of questions that show interest in peers. In Braxton's story, Braxton learned that two other children liked dinosaurs, but he didn't know how to show interest in their lives. The teacher should help him ask questions of Todd and Rashawn rather than just bragging about his own dinosaur collection. To help Braxton generate a list of questions he can use when talking to Todd and Rashawn, the teacher could ask Braxton, "What would you like someone to know about your dinosaur collection?" These questions might help Todd and Rashawn believe that Braxton is interested in their dinosaurs as well as his own. The teacher could post these sample questions so all the children can visit the list when they are struggling with what to say. During group time, role-playing real-life situations that happen in your program helps children learn how to ask questions about things that might matter to potential friends. This is a hard concept for young children to grasp and is a hard skill to learn. It takes time and regular practice for children to understand and use it consistently.

Complimenting others is a foreign concept to preschoolers, and school-age children seldom do it. Even though children like to receive compliments, they don't see the benefit of giving them. Asking children how they feel when they receive compliments is the first step in helping children understand the benefits of giving truthful compliments. The key to an effective compliment is beginning and ending with truthfulness. A compliment also needs to be about something children can relate to, such as "You really make nice pictures," or "I like the way you dance." A compliment circle at group time helps provide children with a variety of compliment ideas as they listen to others give compliments to peers. This activity can provide children with accolades they can use with their own friends in the future.

Children like it when others are kind to them, but they do not always understand why they should be kind to others. Often children can't identify when someone is doing something kind for them. Simple things like sharing the crayons or helping a child pick up the pieces of a dropped puzzle are acts of kindness. But unless an adult labels these actions as kindnesses for the child, how is the child supposed to know? As an adult walks around the play space and notices a child has done a nice thing for someone else, they can make a simple comment about the kindness. For example, a teacher might say, "That was a kind thing to do. I'm sure your friend appreciated it." This type of comment does three things: it labels the action as kindness, it tells the receiver of the kindness that gratitude is in order, and it elevates confidence for the giver. Doing nice things for others makes both the giver and the receiver feel good.

Another important aspect of building friendships is learning how to participate in groups of friends. This skill includes three parts:

- entering into a group
- collaborating as a member of the group
- exiting the group

Children need to know when and how to enter a group. If children are excited about what is going on in the group, they may rush in and disrupt play. This bull-in-a-china-shop approach to entering an existing playgroup can be disastrous for all parties, resulting in hurt feelings and inappropriate behaviors.

Timing is everything. Help children determine the best time to join a playgroup. Children usually have more success entering a group at the beginning of the activity. At this point, children are creating parameters such as the rules and end products. Another possible entry point is when there is a break in the action, such as when one part of the activity is completed and a new one is going to begin. This is a harder entry point for children because they just want to be included, and delaying gratification can be a challenge. Helping children wait for entry often results in success, with acceptance and entry into the groups. A third possible entry point is when the group needs help solving a problem. For example, children who want to gain entry could offer to hand others blocks when they are building a structure or be the cook in dramatic play.

If children enter a group play space that has reached its limit of children, their request will be met with an automatic no. The entering child may not understand that the rejection is not because the group does not want the child to play with them, but rather because there is not enough space. So take time to explain this to the child. To prevent similar misunderstandings in the future, use the strategies of occupancy signs and waiting lists that are explained on pages 54–55 in chapter 3.

Once children know when to enter a group, learning how to greet their peers is the next step. Saying hello to a child and calling the child by name shows respect. Begin teaching this skill by having children work in pairs to practice saying hello to the person they would like to play with, such as saying, "Hi, Sam." Children may find that the person they would like to play with is so engrossed in play that calling their name is not enough to get their attention. They may have to lay a soft hand on the person's shoulder and repeat their greeting. Even if you have already discussed what using soft hands means, children may need to be reminded. It is important that children learn that the touch is a truly soft touch, not a punch in the arm. The touch needs to be followed by the request, such as "Can I play with you? I would like to build a tower too." Entering the group can be tricky business and takes a lot of practice. Help children practice greeting others by having them greet while standing face-to-face, and then have one child turn to face away from the speaker so that the speaker can practice greeting a peer when the peer is not making eye contact. These two types of greetings pull the child's attention away from play and help the child focus on the speaker.

Finally, children must learn how to exit a group. Children may not know how to leave a playgroup without disrupting play. When children leave a group, they often simply walk away from the toys and materials they used, expecting others to pick them up and upsetting the rest of the children in the group. Sometimes children leave abruptly, without telling their play partners, which can cause confusion and disappointment for their peers. You can teach children how to leave a group without disrupting play. First, have the children tell their playmates that they are finished playing. Have them begin putting their materials away. Have them thank the other children for playing with them. Finally, have them leave quietly, without disturbing the remaining play.

Working in a Group

The preceding section discusses working in groups as it relates to friendship building. It is also important for children to learn to work together toward a common goal or to complete a specific task. For children, working in groups can easily become a competition. Children need to remember that the ultimate goal of working in groups is to share the workload. Cooperation allows everyone to pitch in and get the job done. Adults need to create opportunities for children to work together. Here are some examples:

- Put on a play.
- Work on a collective piece of art.
- Plan a party for another class.
- Make drawings or cards for a senior center.
- Create a holiday presentation for family, friends, and community leaders.
- Make a meal together.
- Collect items for donation to a homeless shelter.
- Go to a senior care facility and sing songs.

Preschoolers and schoolagers love these types of projects. Each of these examples offers opportunities for the adult and the children to identify tasks and create work groups responsible for specific tasks. For instance, if the class chooses to make a meal together, the class must first decide on what tasks need to be done to complete the project. Then they must form work groups and assign one group to each task. The task groups could be as follows: decorations, making desserts, setting the table, making the main course and sides, and cleaning up. Each group can decide what needs to be done to complete its assigned task, and who will do what. In a multiage program, include both older and younger children within each group. This approach allows for peer teaching and support.

It is amazing what children learn from a simple project like planning a meal. Children learn to communicate and follow directions as they work side by side, following recipes to make all the parts of the meal. Their creativity takes center stage when they create table decorations. They learn to take responsibility for setting the table so that everyone has what they need and for cleaning up the table after the meal is complete. Each task requires the children to cooperate with one another to accomplish the task. The children learn that by sharing the work, they can accomplish something big together that they couldn't accomplish alone.

Collaboration

Working in a group is how the actual work gets done. Collaboration is the merging of multiple points of view to create a plan of action to complete a project. Collaboration is the foundation for working with others. Children are not born with this skill, so adults must teach it to children.

To collaborate, children need to be open to the ideas and thoughts of others. In the previously described meal-making project, the children on the decorating committee need to decide what the decorations will be. Each member of the decorating work group describes what they would like. Collaboration takes place when the children consider all the ideas presented and decide what the decorations will be and who will be doing what. All the children in the work group need to listen to what is being proposed and participate in making decisions. Finding value in others' opinions and being OK when the group chooses others' ideas are important skills.

Offering a child a choice, such as "You can have milk or juice for lunch," is the beginning of learning two-way communication, speaking, and listening. Being willing to listen when others speak is the foundation for collaboration. It is through listening that children receive information. They may agree or disagree with the information or may find that they do not understand what the speaker is trying to communicate. Armed with information, children can make appropriate comments or ask questions needed for clarification. Becoming a collaborating member of a group requires give-and-take and good communication skills. Chapter 2 discusses in detail the skills needed for positive communication.

Empathy

It is important for children to have friends. Even after children successfully make friends, the real work is in keeping friends—and that requires the development of empathy. Empathy is possessing an understanding of another person's feelings and experiences. Actions associated with empathy are kindness, caring, concern, and sympathy. All children want to be appreciated, and they believe that everyone should be able to recognize when they are upset or feel offended by someone. Children want to be understood, and they desire compassion when they are sad or feel slighted in some way.

Infants exhibit a precursor to empathy when they cry upon hearing other babies cry. Toddlers convey that they have the beginnings of empathy by offering others who are crying a hug or a favorite toy. Most preschoolers can identify feelings they see in others, but preschoolers cannot translate the feelings they see into the feelings they feel. Children ages five to six can understand another person's feelings, display compassion, and desire to help fix the problem.

One of the most important skills in developing empathy is the ability to read body language, which is discussed at length in chapter 2. It is hard to feel empathy for someone else when you have not noticed that they are upset. You can help children develop empathy by helping them understand how body language tells them what others are feeling and when they are in distress. Have children identify the feelings of other people by asking questions like the following:

- What does my face tell you about how I am feeling?
- Joe is moving to a new house. How do you think he feels today?
- Can you show me what your face looks like when you are frustrated?
- When Chloe tripped and fell to the ground, how do you think she felt?
- Today is Matt's birthday, and he brought a special snack. How do you think he feels?
- Cheri threw sand at Samantha today. How do you think that made Samantha feel?

Once children learn to identify feelings, the next step is to help children connect each feeling to a time in their own lives when they felt that way. If possible, include scenarios that may have happened in the program or at home. This strategy helps children self-identify feelings and recall those feelings when another person is experiencing a similar situation. Developing empathy is a long process. It can take well into adulthood to master. For this reason, adults need to be patient with children who are developing empathy. Even small successes should be celebrated.

PROVIDERS' ROLE

Intentional Teaching

Creating a respectful, safe, supportive learning community where all children feel valued and capable is often a time-consuming and messy process. The adult's role is to facilitate this process. Creating this environment requires the intentional planning of activities that teach community-building skills. Adults sometimes do what is easier and faster rather than teach children to be responsible and to act independently without constant reminders. But creating a community where children feel they belong occurs when adults share control of the environment. Planning spaces that children like with activities that interest them engages the children in the community. Making materials accessible to the children so they can get and return materials, toys, and supplies independently teaches them responsibility and encourages their independence.

Adults may feel they are the only ones who know how to create rules to keep children safe. However, adults need to share the responsibility for community rules with members of the community. When adults include children in rulemaking, the children will be more likely to understand and comply with the rules generated. In addition, children will help other children comply by reminding them of the rules. One important step in creating community rules is establishing shared meaning for terms that can be confusing for children, such as *soft hands*, *respect*, and *safe choices*. Because rules set the stage for behavioral expectations, all members of the community need to know and understand what the words in the rules mean and what expectations they establish for members of the community.

Children learn to be independent when they have jobs to do that are age appropriate and easily completed by the child. Completing a job consistently over time can help a child become competent, capable, and confident. Jobs are contributions to the community, so by doing their jobs, children develop ownership within the community.

In addition to jobs, staged activities that teach a skill over time can help children achieve both confidence and competence. Staged activities break down a physical or emotional skill into parts. Each activity builds on the previous activity until the child can use the skill confidently. Children will not be effective at using the skill 100 percent of the time—few people consistently use every social skill. But through time, practice, and experience, most of the time children can call on a specific skill when it's needed.

Children need conversation and usually like to engage in it. Talking *with* children and not *at* them helps children feel valued. Conversations also offer adults opportunities to become aware of children's interests. When adults know these interests, they can help children brainstorm community outreach ideas. Helping young children look to the world outside and find ways to work toward a common goal can help them believe that they are a part of the larger community. Even young preschoolers can go to a senior center and sing songs, plant flowers out in the community or around the center, or participate in a recycling program.

Finding and keeping friends is important in maintaining overall emotional health for all people. Children come from diverse backgrounds, and their social-emotional playing field is not level. Children may understand what they need from others and know that they want friends, but may not know what the benefits of having a friend are and what they need to do to make and keep friends. An adult caregiver needs to help children understand these concepts. Children will sometimes need adults to orchestrate opportunities for them to play together so that friendships have an opportunity to develop. Provide opportunities for children to role-play different friendship skills, such as understanding another person's point of view, the traits of a good friend, and collaborating to find solutions to a problem.

Environment Design

Environmental Elements That Foster Community Building

PHYSICAL ENVIRONMENT	TEMPORAL ENVIRONMENT	INTERPERSONAL ENVIRONMENT
• Gathering area for small- and large-group activities	• Fair and age-appropriate rules, consequences, and limits	• Providing support and guidance to promote cooperation rather than completion
• Well-defined areas for group free play that clearly post occupancy limits	• Scheduled group time to introduce a new skill and update the children on what is new or changed in the program space	• Including children in developing rules and consequences
• Area-specific rules (computer, art, snack, and outdoors) posted in each area	• Jobs that allow children to learn a new age-appropriate skill, such as greeting friends as they enter the room, being an art monitor who determines when the art supplies need to be added, or learning how to properly answer the phone	• Encouraging acceptance
• Comfortable furniture, tables, and chairs, including soft elements when possible	• Greeting the children by name each day	• Encouraging empathy
• Materials, toys, and posters that reflect the diversity of the children		

Strategies for Intentional Teaching and Encouraging Skill Development

- Practice greeting others.
- Pair up children in the program to practice introducing themselves.
- Practice the steps of building a friendship.
- Post child-generated rules and definitions.
- Provide places for children to sit side by side and talk to encourage friendship building.
- Role-play scenarios that help children understand the traits of a good friend.
- Provide opportunities for children to feel a part of the larger community.

PARENT AND STAFF EDUCATION STRATEGIES

Community building starts with a methodology of respect. The environment needs to provide a safe, caring atmosphere for all. Help parents understand this philosophy by posting information within the program handbook, on parent bulletin boards, and on websites. These few simple steps will outline the behavior expectations for children, family members, and staff. Creating consistency in practice and transparent communication will help to establish a buy in of children and their family members. Educate parents about the benefits of and the need for children to develop friendships. Provide tips on friendship building to family members and encourage them to use those tips with their children. Place these tips in the newsletters and on your website and send out email blasts. Helping parents and staff understand what empathy is and encouraging them to model true empathy with others can go a long way in minimizing teasing and bullying within your program. Staff meetings are a great opportunity to educate staff about community building. Intentionally take time within your meetings to discuss community-building strategies. Encourage staff to brainstorm small- and large-group activities that encourage children to become engaged in the program and in the community at large. Have staff evaluate their space and identify existing spaces that will encourage talking and working cooperatively. If none exist, ask them to create spaces that encourage cooperation. Hosting community events such as picnics, parent nights, or game nights for children and families can provide family fun, a sense of community, and information around the topics of friendship, empathy, and collaboration.

Things to Remember

- Do not do for children what they can do for themselves.
- We get better at something only if we practice.
- Make children's safety your first priority.
- Facilitate problem solving only if safety becomes a concern.
- Children need and like to have community jobs.
- Children are not born with collaboration skills.
- Complimenting others can be foreign to children.
- Friendships are important in the lives of children.

Children's Books Dealing with Community Building

- *Big Al* by Andrew Clements
- *The Brand New Kid* by Katie Couric
- *Charlie the Caterpillar* by Dom DeLuise
- *Chrysanthemum* by Kevin Henkes
- *Fly Away Home* by Eve Bunting
- *Good People Everywhere* by Lynea Gillen
- *Have You Filled a Bucket Today?* by Carol McCloud
- *Hooway for Wodney Wat* by Helen Lester
- *I Accept You as You Are!* by David Parker
- *Jilly's Terrible Temper Tantrums: And How She Outgrew Them* by Martha Heineman Pieper
- *Know and Follow Rules* by Cheri J. Meiners
- *Making Choices and Making Friends* by Pamela Espeland and Elizabeth Verdick
- *Making Friends* by Cassie Mayer
- *Margaret and Margarita* by Lynn Reiser
- *A Rainbow of Friends* by P. K. Hallinan
- *That Rule Doesn't Apply to Me!* by Julia Cook
- *Wilma Jean the Worry Machine* by Julia Cook

Conflict Resolution

WHAT IS CONFLICT RESOLUTION?

Conflict resolution is a process in which two or more individuals strive to settle a disagreement in a safe, peaceful way while protecting the rights of all involved. Conflict resolution is sometimes referred to as problem solving. These terms are often used interchangeably. For adult caregivers, conflict resolution involves multiple strategies, including environment design, age-appropriate materials and supplies, and intentional teaching of problem-solving skills.

Children learn how to handle conflict from what they see and experience in everyday life. When conflict arises, children typically react in one of three ways. Some will walk away and remove themselves from the conflict. Others will talk their way through a conflict. Still others will melt down—emotionally, behaviorally, or both. They may cry, kick, scream, hit, or shove others.

The Causes of Conflict

So how can you avert a meltdown? First and foremost, understand that you cannot prevent or eliminate all conflict in a child's life. You can control only the time the child spends in your program. And even in your program, you cannot expect a conflict-free zone. Children are human beings, and humans have disagreements. You can, however, take a proactive approach to conflict rather than a reactive one. Approaching conflict proactively begins with your program's environment design and the amount and types of materials within the program space. If you can create an environment where children have ample space and adequate age-appropriate materials and supplies, then you'll remove one major cause of conflict among children.

Keep in mind that things may happen outside your program that cause children stress, which increases the potential for conflict. To get a handle on stress-induced conflict, begin by asking family members if they can identify things that trigger their children to melt down. Most children have triggers that spark conflict with others. Together you and the family can identify behavioral patterns that indicate conflict triggers. Ask yourselves the following questions about specific conflicts and multiple conflicts:

- What happened right before the conflict?
- Who was in the playgroup?
- What time did the conflict occur?
- What was the conversation between the children before the conflict occurred?
- What was each child's version of what happened?
- Is there anything (event, person, object, or activity) that consistently seems to trigger conflict for a specific child?

Once you have identified triggers, it will be easier to prevent crises. Remember, though, that even when you have identified triggers, your prevention efforts will not always work. As children grow and as other children enter and exit the program, triggers may change. Existing triggers may fade as children learn to cope with specific stressors, while new triggers may appear.

A few common triggers are being touched by other children, having others sit in one's chair, or hearing loud noises. To minimize these triggers, you can help other children understand that the child does not like to be touched, that the child needs to sit in his or her own chair, or that loud noises upset the child. For the child who does not like to be touched, help other children understand the idea of personal space. Use a small Hula-Hoop or have the children extend their arms out to the sides to give the children a visual representation of personal space. For the child who must always sit in a particular chair, take time to explain to other children why the child needs to sit in a specific chair and encourage the children to sit side by side. For the child who hates loud noises, provide noise-canceling headphones or use earmuffs to minimize noises. Conflict-prevention strategies should be tailored to the specific children involved. If the adults take the time to explain such modifications, most children will understand the other child's needs and will comply.

In one child care program, the teacher mentioned frustration over conflicts in the game area. The teacher was perplexed. She said, "I have tried everything, from offering no games to putting out many different kinds of games." I asked about the age range of the children in the program. The teacher responded, "From three to six years old." I asked if the children had ever mentioned what types of games they liked to play, and she answered, "No." During the next group time, she asked the children what games they liked to play, and she charted their answers.

After comparing the charted answers to the games in the classroom, several things were evident to the teacher. First, the games were in poor shape. Pieces were everywhere, sending the message that the games were unimportant and the children need not take care of them. Second, the age range of the games did not match the ages of children in the program. Finally, only one game in the game area was on the child-generated list.

The teacher took steps to match the materials and supplies in the game area more effectively to the needs and interests of the children. She provided enough games to give the children choices without overwhelming them. She placed a "lost pieces" container in the game area to discourage children from placing stray pieces on the floor or in the garbage. She redesigned the space to include a table with four chairs, to signify that the space was meant for four children. She put a bookshelf in the space to provide both game storage and easy access for the children. She revamped the game collection, providing games for children ages two to seven years old. She chose this age range purposefully, to both meet the needs of the children and create a challenge to help expand their learning potential. The games provided were a fifty-fifty mix of child-generated ideas and adult-chosen games. She started rotating 50 percent of the games every week to spark continued interest in this area while maintaining some familiarity. The teacher noted that only one week after she revamped the space, conflict in that area decreased markedly.

If conflict is occurring regularly in a specific area, take time to assess the environment and the materials. Determine if the conflict occurs because the space does not provide what the children need to be successful. Make this kind of investigation part of your weekly environment checklist to help minimize future conflicts.

Just like children, adults have conflict triggers. They may react strongly when children behave in a certain way. Some adults may see these behaviors as unintentional mistakes, while others see the behaviors as intentional or as evidence of a character flaw. Taking the latter view can lead to further problems. According to social psychologist David W. Johnson and educator Roger T. Johnson (1996), "There are potentially numerous negative outcomes of poorly managed conflicts, including lower achievement and detrimental effects on individual students such as stress and challenges to self-esteem and self-efficacy." By contrast, taking the position that problematic behaviors are unintentional mistakes can help teachers redirect these behaviors toward a positive outcome.

Conflict in the Media

Children are bombarded with many images throughout the day, from TV, gaming systems, mobile apps, the internet, and more. They are receiving information all the time, but they do not have enough life experience or knowledge to understand all the implications of such information. Young children are often unable to tell the difference between fantasy and reality, and the violent images they see on these platforms tend to further confuse children. Every day, TV, the internet, radio, and print news tell of shootings, drug deals, domestic violence, and other distressing events. While reporting news, the media tell children how some people deal with problems. Often these solutions are negative examples of problem solving. This exposure can negatively affect children's ability to solve problems in appropriate physically and emotionally safe ways. According to the Council on Communications and Media (COCM), "Extensive research evidence indicates that media violence can contribute to aggressive behavior, desensitization to violence, nightmares, and fear of being harmed" (2009).

How does this happen? Children are inundated with images, words, and attitudes that reinforce the idea that "I am bigger; therefore I am right" and "I can push you and take what I want, and that is OK." With the increasing exposure to negative examples of problem solving, children's ability to solve problems peacefully is declining. To combat this trend, adults need to intentionally teach effective problem-solving strategies.

Young children learn early that they can play the same electronic game over and over again. As children grow, their interest in gaming increases, and the content of their games expands. Even the simplest games require the player to achieve increasingly difficult levels. Older preschoolers and school-agers find themselves playing games in which they must collect coins or points to complete a level and move up to the next level. What they have to do to collect those points varies, from driving a car down a path, to hopping from tower to tower, to shooting balls at characters in the game to eliminate those characters. Some games use weapons like swords and fireballs to eliminate characters from the game and allow the player to move forward and get a reward. Children learn that when a character is eliminated, a quick reboot of the game brings the character back, as good as new.

When adults allow unfettered access to gaming, they are giving their blessing for the content and saying without words that it is OK to do the things portrayed in the games and solve problems in the same manner. Children may get the message that if they don't want to deal with someone, then the solution is to remove them. When a child eliminates a character in a game, the character returns when the child reboots the game; however, when someone is eliminated in real life, the person does not return. Children may not understand that the fantasy world of gaming works differently from the real world.

Caring adults in the lives of children must help children understand the realities of violence and help them learn that better options exist. You can consciously modify what you watch, read, and do in the presence of children and monitor what children see and play while they use electronic devices. You should also help children distinguish fantasy from reality.

You can discuss real-life situations to help children understand the differences between reality and fantasy. Start with a real occurrence that the children remember and that was not easily fixed. This will help them connect the dots. For instance, have the children think of when a child got injured or when something got damaged in the program. You might say, "Remember when Mayling broke her arm on the playground? When she came back to school after going to the doctor, was her arm all better?" Or you might ask, "Remember when our water pipe burst, and we had water all over the floor, and we had to move to Ms. Jan's room? We wanted to be back in our own room, but it took a long time to get things fixed." In addition, you could read a fiction book involving animals that talk, then ask, "Do animals talk like we do?" When children ask questions or talk about a pet dying, this, too, could be a teachable moment about things that happen in the real world. Use such moments to talk about reality versus fantasy. Another strategy might be to introduce children to community helpers, such as police officers and firefighters. These helpers can talk about the realities of their jobs. Provide time for children to ask questions. These questions will vary based on the ages of the children. Preschoolers may want to look at the fire truck or the police car. Schoolagers may want to know particulars about the job and ask about something they heard an adult talk about or saw on TV. Asking questions helps children process what they have seen or heard and distinguish between the reality of the work and the picture painted on-screen.

Problem Solving

The best protection for children against the harsh realities of life is learning nonviolent ways to solve problems. When children are in conflict, your job is to focus on talking through the problem, to try to understand their point of view, and to determine a compromise or solution on which all parties agree. And you need to plan intentional activities that help children practice peaceful conflict resolution.

Learning problem solving takes time. Anything worth learning usually does. Young children may have a difficult time solving problems peacefully on their own because they do not yet have the experience or skills to do so. So teaching them options besides violence is a top priority. The following scenario offers an example of showing children that they have nonviolent options for problem solving.

> Several children were running around in the outdoor play space. Joshua, Simon, Clinton, and Penny were playing at the water table. The water table was located on a flat, grassy area. The table was equipped with waterwheels, strainers, cups, bowls, and spoons.

The noise level in this area started to rise. The teacher moved closer to the table to listen in on the children's conversation. The children were talking about how the water made the waterwheel turn.

Joshua said, "I can make it go faster with my bowl."

Penny grabbed the bowl from Joshua and started to pour water on the waterwheel. Joshua and Penny started pulling the bowl back and forth.

Simon said, "Give it back, Penny."

The teacher said, "It looks like you need some help. I will hold the bowl until we can decide what to do with it." The teacher asked each child what happened. Simon eagerly defended Joshua. After all the children had their say, the teacher recapped the story out loud to make sure she understood both the events and the associated feelings. She said to Penny, "It was really exciting to see how fast the wheel spun when Joshua poured water over it from his bowl, and you wanted to try it—but Joshua was sad when you took the bowl from him. What else could you have done so you could have a turn with the bowl?" Guiding the conversation onward, the teacher was able to confirm what had happened and why the children had a problem, but she turned the problem-solving responsibility back to the children.

Penny was very quiet. Joshua said to her, "You could have just asked me for a turn."

The teacher asked Penny how she might ask Joshua for a turn. Together they practiced asking for a turn. The teacher said, "I am going to give the bowl back to Joshua now, and when you want a turn, you can ask Joshua."

The teacher stayed near the water table and watched as the children played. Penny asked for a turn, and Joshua gave her one.

Through the entire process, Clinton was present but said very little. As the play progressed, Clinton wanted the slotted spoon that Penny had. He asked for a turn, just as the children had practiced with their teacher, and Penny gave the spoon to Clinton without incident.

This type of tug-of-war is common in any school or child care program with multiple children. The teacher in this scenario handled it skillfully, interrupting the conflict before someone could be hurt. She then identified the item that was in contention. Holding that item so the children could see it while they talked about their problem-solving options let the children know that the bowl would be returned to the water table when they agreed on a compromise.

Helping children find peaceful ways to resolve conflict is a gift for a lifetime. Conflict-resolution skills will serve children well as they grow older. They can use these skills in their personal, academic, and business lives, helping them become productive members of society.

Following are several strategies you can use to minimize conflict in your program:

- Identify the situations and objects that trigger conflicts among children.
- Evaluate spaces where conflict consistently occurs to determine whether something (or the lack of something) in the activity space needs to be changed.
- Provide enough materials and supplies for the number of children allowed within each activity area.
- Share a children's book that portrays problems similar to those occurring in your program to start a conversation about peaceful problem-solving strategies children can use.
- Limit children's screen time.
- Monitor what children are watching and playing on all media devices.
- Minimize access to toys, movies, games, TV shows, and internet content that portray violence.

The remainder of this chapter will discuss the skills that work cooperatively to help a person resolve conflict peacefully.

ASSOCIATED SKILLS

Aversion to Violence

Children have a natural aversion to violence. They will often cover their eyes if something scary happens on-screen when they are watching a show. They will cover their ears when they hear loud noises, such as fireworks or yelling. They will duck if they feel something is going to hit them. Some children may enjoy the thrill of a scary amusement park ride, but they do not typically want to be a part of something they feel will hurt them. No one likes to be hurt, either physically or emotionally. However, as we've discussed earlier in this chapter, children may become slowly desensitized to violence or accept violence as a part of life through exposure to violence in the media and in the world. Your role is to help the children in your care turn away from violence as a way to solve their problems or get what they want. When children choose violence to solve a problem, the consequence—intended or unintended—of that choice is physical and emotional harm.

Keep in mind that we all get mad. Teach children that it is OK to get mad, but there are things that they can and cannot do when they get mad. Children can tell someone they are mad. They can sit in a quiet place when they are mad and think before they speak. They can write in a journal about their feelings and describe what happened to make them so mad. You should also teach children what they cannot do when they are mad. It is not OK to hit or yell at people and pets, nor is it OK to destroy property or throw things, such as blocks or crayons.

It can be difficult to teach children the benefits of not choosing violence. When children are managing their own screen time or can freely surf the internet and download images and games, they may become confused about how to solve problems and whether violence is appropriate. It looks so easy on-screen, and gratification is immediate. It may be best to start at the beginning whenever conflict occurs. Refer to the community rules, and remind children that everyone must be safe within your community. Sometimes this is a hard thing for children to remember when they are angry. Continue by explaining that when unkind words are said or blocks are thrown, children may get hurt, and that is not allowed. Help children see that they have other options, and help them understand the results of each option. This approach teaches children to weigh all options before they act.

Negotiation

In negotiation, the people involved bargain with one another. They communicate back and forth, presenting their positions and listening to the positions of others, looking for common ground. Children are born negotiators. They try to negotiate for another snack, a new toy, a later bedtime, and so on.

Good negotiation skills are essential in life. Children who possess good negotiation skills increase their confidence and improve their relationships. To be good negotiators, children need the ability to display genuine empathy and collaborate. A good negotiator goes into a negotiation with a request but follows with reasons why the request is good. To negotiate successfully, children must think ahead about what the other party might consider a valid reason to enter into an agreement and what they would view as the downside to the agreement. Adults will always consider some things nonnegotiable, but allowing children to make a case for doing something out of the norm whenever possible can teach them a lot.

In preschoolers, negotiation can look like conflict. Even in a conflict, children who are good negotiators are those who are ready with a solution. That solution may be one-sided, and the adult may consider it unfair to the other child. However, if all children involved agree on the solution, then the adult should step back and let it play out. The adult should try to focus on the learning that is taking place rather than on what seems fair.

In a preschool classroom there were sixteen children, a lead teacher, and a classroom aide. During free-choice time, Jason and Ricky were sitting side by side putting together separate marble runs. Each child had a box of loops, troughs, and tubes for the marbles to roll down and through, ending up at the bottom of the run. Each child began with a small run made of three or four pieces. As the play extended and the children became more confident, the runs became taller and more complex and used more pieces.

Jason wanted to add another piece to his marble run. He found that in his box, he did not have any more of the type of piece he wanted. He asked Ricky if he could have the desired piece from Ricky's box.

Ricky said, "It is the last one. I want to use it."

Jason thought for a moment and said, "How about we trade? I will give you these two pieces if you give me that one."

Ricky was still not convinced.

Jason then said, "Can I just borrow the piece and use it once? Then I will give it right back."

Ricky let Jason borrow the piece. Jason tried it and then gave the piece back to Ricky.

These two boys were friends and played together often. Jason did not stop negotiating with Ricky after the first refusal. Jason just kept making offers until he found an offer Ricky could live with.

This scenario could have ended much differently—and scenarios like this often do. Sometimes adults intervene and try to impose their idea of fairness on negotiations. Witnessing negotiation between children can be painful for an adult if the adult feels it is unfair to one child. But intervention in the name of fairness isn't always the best course of action. Children should come up with their own ideas and then see the results of the negotiation. Adults must know when to jump in and when to let a negotiation play out. To determine when to jump in, first consider the safety of the children. If you question the safety of the children, stop the action but encourage the children to solve the problem. If the children are not in danger, take the position of the observer and see how the children use their negotiation skills to solve the problem. Standing nearby when children are negotiating is always a good idea, but many negotiations take place without an adult present.

Jason's negotiation with Ricky took several offers before the boys found one that was acceptable to both of them. Jason's first attempt did not succeed, but he did not give up; he kept trying different ideas to get what he wanted. His final offer allowed both boys to use the desired piece. Jason got it for a short time, while Ricky maintained ownership. The teacher could have stepped in and imposed a solution but instead allowed the boys to be the negotiators.

Negotiation among schoolagers can be a great learning experience. Even kindergarteners are quick to offer opinions and solutions.

In a school-age summer program, children ages five to eight were put into four mixed-age groups and were given the task of determining what field trips they would like to take over the summer. An adult was assigned to each group. The adult's role was to facilitate the group's negotiations and act as a scribe. The adults monitored their groups to maximize learning and to make sure that even the youngest children gave input. They answered questions, did the math, and directed the children to resources. They did not offer opinions, intervene in negotiations, or steer the selection of field trips.

The teachers told the children the number of students in the summer program, the amount of money in the budget for summer field trips, the cost of busing for each trip, and a list of the trips taken in previous summers. Each group's task was to come up with a list of twelve field trips, including the cost per student for each trip, and the list needed to stay within the budget. The teachers told the children that each group would present its list to the other groups.

Within each group, the adult asked every child where he or she would like to go on a field trip and charted the answers. Then each group reviewed all its members' answers, chose a list of twelve field trips, and tabulated the total cost.

Each group presented its list to the other groups. The children spoke passionately about their choices. After all the groups shared their lists, the children spotted some similarities, so they worked together to make a new list composed of field trips chosen by most of the groups. They tallied the cost of this list and found that there was money left over in the budget. The children looked at the remaining suggestions on the original group lists for one additional trip. It was not long before the children homed in on a trip to the local amusement park, but it did not fit in the budget.

A few days later, the children asked to talk about the field trips again. They had come up with a plan to raise the additional money needed for the amusement park trip. They outlined their fundraising plan and explained the many learning activities they could do in the classroom prior to the field trip and while they were at the amusement park.

The adults could have just said no to an additional field trip when the children discovered it was over budget, but instead the adults encouraged the children to come up with a solution to this problem. Over the next few days, the adults allowed the children to do the research and the math needed to persuade them. By allowing this, they enabled the children to learn and practice good negotiation skills: knowing their limits, doing their research, and coming back to the table prepared to answer questions, debate their position, and abide by agreements made through the negotiation.

Chapter 5

In this scenario, the children knew that the money was the issue, so they had to identify the choices that were available to them. Through some discussion, they determined that their three options were eliminating one other field trip to go to the amusement park, forgetting about the amusement park, or finding additional funds to go to the amusement park. They worked together to create a plan. Through this project, they better understood the real costs of field trips and accepted that as much as the teachers wanted to add an amusement park trip, the school simply couldn't afford it. The problem forced the children to be creative and think about other points of view and possible solutions to their problem.

While the staff orchestrated this lesson on negotiation, negotiation among children can also occur spontaneously. Letting children negotiate for more free choice, specific field trips, what clothes they wear, when they go to bed, or when they do their homework lets them know their opinions matter and their ideas and feelings are respected.

Resolution Strategies

Teaching resolution strategies should begin at an early age. Even preschoolers can master the art of resolution. When children use resolution strategies, they employ a mix of social skills and work together to find a solution that is acceptable to all parties. In previous chapters, we have discussed control, coping skills, and delaying gratification. Each of these skills helps children get to a place where they can think about a resolution to a conflict.

Conflict is a part of daily life—and resolving conflict should be too. Resolution occurs when both parties are willing to resolve the conflict. Control skills help stop the action before the situation escalates. Intentionally stopping the action enables children to delay gratification until they reach a solution. Once the action is stopped, the next step is to manage negative feelings associated with the issue at hand by using coping and de-stressing skills to calm down.

The philosophy of any child care program or school needs to be that of a peaceable community. It must be a place where children value peace, respect one another, are willing to understand another person's point of view, and can be empathetic toward their peers and family members. In a peaceable community, conflict is minimized and friendships flourish.

Schools and child care programs with a peaceable methodology may use a peace table as a resolution strategy. A peace table is a place children can go that is set aside expressly for the purpose of calming down and solving conflict. A peace table should be placed in a quiet corner of the room. It should be equipped with two chairs, and both the table and chairs should be used only for the peace table. (Alternatively, two beanbags on a carpet in a quiet corner may serve as a peace "table.") The peace table should also include an item that can be held by the child speaking, such as a bear or stress ball. If you are currently using a speaker's prop to teach listening skills in other areas of the program, children will be familiar with this concept.

When you introduce a peace table, you'll need to explain to the children how it works. Do this during group time. Start by discussing listening skills. Introduce the speaker's prop and explain how to use it. Then play a simple game. Pass the prop around the circle, and as each child holds the prop, they can tell the group about a favorite food. Have the rest of the group listen, then repeat back what the child said. Follow up this game by role-playing typical real-life conflicts with another adult. As a group, talk about the conflict and chart the children's ideas for how to handle it. If a child says, "That happened to me," use it as a teachable moment. Validate the child's experience and have the child tell how they felt, both physically and emotionally. Don't worry about children hijacking the lesson, because personal stories help children self-identify their feelings and understand how others might feel in a similar situation. Repeat this activity many times over a few weeks to help cement the process in children's minds.

When a conflict arises between two children, one of the children can invite the other to the peace table to resolve the conflict. The inviting child gets to speak first, while the other child listens. Then the children change roles. Once the children have both told their stories, they can generate a list of solutions. Together they can choose a potential solution. Once the conflict is resolved, both parties can hold the speaker's prop together and declare the peace. They might say something like "We now have peace." The children can then resume play.

To support children's independent resolution of problems, post prompts in words and pictures near the peace table. These prompts can help children through the process and provide a resource if they get stuck. For an example of peace table prompts with pictures, see appendix B. Here is the basic process:

1. Child 1 invites child 2 to the peace table.
2. Child 1 tells their story while child 2 listens.
3. Child 2 tells their story while child 1 listens.

4. Both children generate a list of possible solutions.

5. Both children agree on a solution.

6. The children declare peace together.

7. The children return to play.

At first an adult may need to mediate this process until the children get used to it. This will take time. Repeat role-playing the process regularly to remind children of how it works and to introduce the process to new students.

This is a simple version of peer mediation suitable for preschoolers. As children grow and attend elementary school, they can learn a more formal peer mediation process. A designated adult should be the coordinator and oversee the training of the peer mediators. Peer mediators should represent a cross-section of the student population. The coordinator should train peer mediators in how to facilitate conflict resolution among other children. Children who teach others how to resolve problems become good problem solvers themselves.

Another strategy for schoolagers is to provide writing prompts at a writing table or within individual children's journals. Such prompts allow children to generate a list of ideas or identify feelings they might feel if they were in a suggested situation. For an example of how these prompts might look, see appendix C. To introduce the prompts, ask "How would you feel if" or "What would you do if" the following happened:

- Someone ripped your picture.
- Someone knocked down your building.
- Someone took your toy.
- Someone shoved you down.
- You spilled your milk.
- Someone called you a name.
- Someone yelled at you.
- Someone hit you.
- Your ice-cream cone fell on the floor.

Being empathetic to others' feelings and ideas can help create solutions that all parties can live with, even when they do not get what they want. When children understand one another's points of view (that is, demonstrate empathy), it is easier to believe that their feelings are valued, and therefore easier to compromise and problem solve.

PROVIDERS' ROLE

Intentional Teaching

When conflict occurs among children, adults tend to focus on the conflict itself and not what happened before the conflict or the children's conflict resolution (or lack thereof). When adults are missing this information, they may assume that children are being intentionally disruptive. And without complete information about the incident and an understanding of children's skills, it is hard to plan appropriately to prevent and resolve conflicts. To teach conflict resolution skills, adults must address both the children's behaviors and the program environment.

Conflict among children is often a result of children not getting what they want or frustration about not being able to complete something as effectively as they expected. Begin by understanding which conflict resolution skills children have and which they need to learn. Once you have identified these, create teacher-led activities to improve children's ability to resolve conflict. Encourage children to participate in conflict resolution role-playing activities. Help children develop a process to deal with conflict and display the steps of the process as a reminder. Practice this process with individuals and as a whole group. Be sure to practice conflict resolution strategies when children are not in conflict. Mastery does not happen overnight. Patience, practice, and consistency are the keys to unlocking a child's ability to problem solve effectively. Developmental psychologist Dr. Becky A. Bailey (2015), author of the book *Conscious Discipline: Building Resilient Classrooms*, contends that a child must practice a skill in context two thousand times before it becomes a natural response.

Take time to look at the areas within your program space to determine where conflict takes place. Determine whether the materials and supplies match the needs of the number of children allowed within each activity area. Take time to figure out what you need to add or change to minimize conflict in each area. Include the children in setting clear rules for the area and post them in both words and pictures so that both readers and nonreaders can understand the behavior expectations. Be consistent with enforcing the rules so children feel safe and feel that everyone is treated fairly. Create a space where children can discuss conflicts, and encourage child-generated solutions. Create an accepting and respectful environment to reduce bullying. Monitor online access and teach appropriate online safety strategies. Help children learn the art of negotiation and provide opportunities for them to practice these skills.

Integrating resolution strategies in your program and being consistent with enforcing rules while maintaining a respectful environment provide a foundation on which children can build conflict resolution skills.

Environment Design

Environmental Elements That Foster Conflict Resolution

PHYSICAL ENVIRONMENT	TEMPORAL ENVIRONMENT	INTERPERSONAL ENVIRONMENT
• Providing multiples of materials and toys so that more than one child can play at the same time	• Creating and posting age-appropriate rules with child-defined terms	• Staff guidance in making connections between previous experiences and new events
• Conflict resolution center, or peace table, that provides space to work through problems	• Providing resources to help children work through their problems	• Problem-solving strategies, such as breathing deeply before acting
		• Encouraging children to take control of their own behavior
		• Encouraging children to come up with other things they could have done that would have a different outcome

Strategies for Intentional Teaching and Encouraging Skill Development

- Role-play problem-solving scenarios.
- Include children in developing community rules.
- Encourage children to define terms used in the community rules, such as *kind hands*, *respect*, and so on.
- Create a problem-solving process.
- Teach children the steps to solving problems.
- Teach school-age children to become peer mediators.
- Identify individual children's conflict triggers and minimize them whenever possible.
- Include the children in designing their space.
- Encourage children to generate their own solutions to conflict.

PARENT AND STAFF EDUCATION STRATEGIES

Ensuring that children and staff alike have good conflict resolution skills and strategies is the foundation of a peaceful program. Each of the following strategies can help create consistency in education and implementation. Because children learn from those around them, it is important that the staff be trained in conflict resolution. This training should not be a one-time event but rather an ongoing part of professional development. Open up these training opportunities to children's family members so families can learn about appropriate ways to deal with conflict too. Make sure that your program handbook clearly explains your program's behavior management system. Remind staff, parents, and families about your program's behavior management system several times a year. Update the program website to reflect conflict resolution strategies and explain how staff will handle conflicts among children. Provide parents and staff with articles that support appropriate conflict resolution strategies for children.

Things to Remember

- Keep in mind that you can minimize conflict, but you can't eliminate it.
- Practice conflict resolution strategies when everyone is calm.
- Know your triggers.
- Provide age-appropriate materials and supplies.
- Remember that children do not like violence.
- Minimize screen time.
- Monitor what children are watching and playing on electronic devices.
- Teach good negotiation skills to increase confidence and improve relationships.
- Encourage children to learn self-soothing, calming, and de-stressing skills.
- Identify triggers that cause children to act inappropriately.

Children's Books Dealing with Conflict Resolution

- *The Chocolate-Covered-Cookie Tantrum* by Deborah Blumenthal
- *The Doorbell Rang* by Pat Hutchins
- *Good People Everywhere* by Lynea Gillen
- *It's Mine!* by Leo Lionni
- *Just Kidding* by Trudy Ludwig
- *Llama Llama Time to Share* by Anna Dewdney
- *One of Each* by Mary Ann Hoberman
- *What Do You Do with an Idea?* by Kobi Yamada
- *What Do You Do with a Problem?* by Kobi Yamada
- *When Sophie Gets Angry—Really, Really Angry . . .* by Molly Bang

CHAPTER 6

Confidence

WHAT IS CONFIDENCE?

Confidence is having a positive and realistic opinion of one's abilities based on one's successes, big and small. It would be great if all children believed in their ability to succeed at all they try. But in reality, people often lack confidence in their ability to do things they wish to do. This lack of confidence may be related to mind-set.

A person's *mind-set* is his or her belief about how the brain is wired and how flexible and able to change the brain is. Stanford University psychologist Carol Dweck (2008b) coined two terms in her book titled *Mindset: The New Psychology of Success* that describe what she believes are the two basic mind-sets people possess: *fixed mind-set* and *growth mind-set*. A fixed mind-set is a belief that one is born with a predetermined set of intelligence and abilities, and these are unchangeable. A growth mind-set is a belief that one's intelligence and abilities can be changed through effort and practice (Mercer and Ryan 2010). Cultivating a growth mind-set in children is key to their development of confidence. According to educator Shelby Pawlina and preschool director Christie Stanford (2011), "When children have episodes of successful learning and of overcoming challenges, they gather evidence that they have the power to influence the outcome of a situation."

For children to feel successful, have positive self-esteem, and feel loved, they first need to feel safe. Safe environments encourage children to try new things and to keep going when the first try doesn't result in mastery. Children are accepted as they are and encouraged to learn from failed experiments. Adults listen to children's activity suggestions and include areas of children's interest in the program space. When children feel safe, they are more likely to try new things and find that they really can do them.

Start from where children are in their levels of confidence and bring them to where you want them to be. To know where to begin, you need to know how children feel about their ability to succeed. Children need to feel that they can be successful; however, it is hard to think of yourself as successful when you are afraid to try. In chapter 1, we discussed how temperament can affect the way children interact with their environment and their peers. Be mindful of a fearful temperament in children. When children have a fearful temperament, it is hard for them to enter a playgroup or new game.

To help children develop a growth mind-set, adults must look at mistakes as opportunities to learn and try alternate strategies. Help children realize that everyone makes mistakes and that mistakes can be the springboard to make another choice or decision that leads to new knowledge or skills. You may observe a defeatist attitude, or a fixed mind-set, in children. For example, a child might say, "I'm not good at that." When you spot this attitude, address it. Use encouraging words to describe the effort expended on a task and the level of success achieved. Truthful and sincere assessment of a job well done helps children believe in their abilities.

When children face challenges and have trouble successfully completing a task or solving a problem, it is OK for them to take a few minutes to be sad. But a few minutes is enough. Dwelling on frustration limits children's ability to move forward and solve the problem. Encourage children to try again. Concentrate on the effort. Encourage practice.

Supportive adults are essential in the lives of children. In an attempt to be supportive, adults often use praise as a way to get children to try again or not feel bad. Praise is fine, but remember that all praise is not equal. Know the difference between truthful praise, which is helpful, and false praise, which is not. Truthful praise comments on actual things children have done, their attitude during the event, and the solutions they've generated. It points out real success and lays the foundation for further progress. False praise makes children feel good without articulating specific skills or achievements. It can allow children to believe they have abilities they do not yet have, creating disappointment later.

Children can have abilities in many things. They can be good at math, gymnastics, problem solving, or empathy. Not every child will be good at everything. It is important for adults to help children understand that all people have things they are good at and things they are not good at. Not everyone will grow up to be a renowned playwright or artist. But that is no reason not to participate in activities for which one has no exceptional talent—for example, children may like to participate in art projects because art is fun and relaxing. Adults can encourage such participation and effort by saying something like "You really worked hard on that picture," or "You really took your time coloring that picture and stayed in the lines." When children struggle with their abilities in a particular area, encouraging the effort instead of the mastery helps children identify the progress they are making toward proficiency and increases their confidence.

Setting goals can also help children raise their confidence level. However, these goals need to be attainable. If a child's goal is to become a basketball star, help the child understand that this is a long-term goal. Explain that shorter-term goals, like getting on a basketball team or being able to make seven out of ten baskets from the foul line, will move the child closer to achieving the long-term goal.

Children often take other people's feedback about their abilities to heart. This can be either constructive or devastating for children, depending on the feedback. Donald Clifton, the grandfather of strengths psychology and coauthor of the book *How Full Is Your Bucket?* (Rath and Clifton 2004), asserts that each person carries an invisible bucket through life and collects in it information from others about how others feel about them. Clifton says that when people say and do things that decrease positive emotions, they are bucket dippers; they diminish others and themselves. Conversely, when people say and do things that increase positive emotions, they are bucket fillers; they fill others' buckets and their own.

All children are bucket dippers sometimes. They usually become dippers because they are hungry, angry, lonely, or tired. Once you know this, it is easier to provide support and skill development to help them become bucket fillers.

Teach children how to be bucket fillers by creating opportunities for them to help others. Also have children create a list of things they believe they are good at. Add skills you know they are good at to help children see themselves as others see them. Often people feel they are not good at something while others think they excel at it. Teach children positive self-talk. When children struggle, self-talk can help them get over their frustration at past failures and try again. Children can repeat to themselves, "I am a good person," or "I am good at science," or "I am a good helper," or "I can do this." Such positive self-talk helps children reaffirm their own worth, encourages them to tackle their problems, and builds their confidence.

Another way to help children become bucket fillers is by accompanying and supporting them until they feel confident. For example, children may want to play a game but not believe they know how, so they sit on the sidelines. If an adult joins them and plays the game with them, they eventually feel less vulnerable and will join in the game with the other children. The adult should play with the children until they are confident about how to play and encourage other children to play. Then, when play is established, the adult should back out of play. Backing out sends the message that the adult believes that the children can now play independently.

ASSOCIATED SKILLS

Positive Self-Image

The Cleveland Clinic describes self-image as how children feel about themselves and their abilities. Self-image develops over time and is built upon how children label their roles in the events in their lives. They may view their role within any event as either a success or a failure. This image may be different from how others see them. There are two schools of thought about the relationship between self-image and life events. Some people believe that one's self-image defines how well or poorly one does in relationships, school, work, and other endeavors. Others believe that life events shape one's self-image. Both schools of thought have merit. When children approach an event or relationship with confidence, more often than not they will be successful and ultimately increase their confidence. Conversely, if children approach the same event or relationship without confidence, their nervousness may reduce their level of success and ultimately reduce their confidence.

As a caring adult, you can help children believe that they can handle whatever comes their way. When they stumble or have a problem, remind them that they can solve the problem with enough time, effort, and support; in other words, foster a growth mind-set. Encourage self-talk, such as "I got this" or "If I keep trying, I will get this," so that children start to believe in their abilities. For children who are struggling with their self-image, adults and peers can help repaint the picture, as in the following scenario.

In one school-age program, several children were struggling with self-image. The teacher faced a constant chorus of "I can't" and "They will think I am dumb." The teacher tried to help the children see their many skills and talents. But often when he talked to a child about their achievements, the child would mention another classmate who had done better.

This habit gave the teacher an idea. He created an activity in which the children complimented one another without putting themselves down. He gave each child a cardboard paper towel tube to decorate. The children wrote their names on their tubes. He provided slips of paper that read, "I like _____ because _____ is really good at _____." Over a two-week period, the teacher encouraged children to fill out one slip for each of their classmates. He assisted children who could not write. He collected the slips as children completed them.

At the end of the two weeks, the teacher gave each child the compliments written by his or her classmates to read and share with others. Most of the children were surprised to realize that so many people had such nice things to say about them. After the children read their compliments, they placed the slips of paper in their decorated tubes and put the tubes in their cubbies. The teacher encouraged the children to reread the compliments whenever they needed a confidence booster.

You can adapt this activity for use in a preschool program. Over the course of several days, work with the children to identify what they like about each child in the classroom. Give each child one sheet of paper for each classmate. Each classmate's sheet can have a different child's picture at the top. Call the children one at a time and ask the children what they like about the child pictured on each sheet of paper. Write down what the children say. Give the children time to draw pictures on each sheet of paper. Write the artist's name on each sheet. Collect all the sheets and create a book for each child. Keep the books in the children's cubbies to be used whenever the children get sad or frustrated.

This type of activity can help children both see where they excel and begin to believe in their own abilities. Many children hear mostly negative comments instead of comments that celebrate their successes. If children hear mostly comments that tell them how bad they are, they lower their expectations and their efforts to match. When you see positive attributes in children, you should tell them, because children may not believe they have those attributes. When you are discussing what children do well, come to the discussion with clear examples that lead you to your conclusion. It is important to help children understand that everyone has talents and areas of strength and that different people have different talents and different degrees of strength.

When children say, "I can't do it," you will first need to determine if they have the physical or mental ability to do the task in question. Is there something outside their control that limits their ability to do the task successfully? If no such barrier exists, then encourage children to try, and tell them you will stay close in case they need help. Introduce the word *yet* to help children see that while they may not be able to do something *yet*, they can get better at the task with practice and effort. So "I cannot read" becomes "I cannot read *yet*." "I cannot catch a ball" becomes "I cannot catch a ball *yet*." This type of reframing helps children realize that their abilities can change, turning a fixed mind-set into a growth mind-set.

Sometimes children will say "I can't" because they want an adult to do a task for them. Let's face it, if someone else does it, then it is easier. An adult may need to sit by them as they try, and offer encouragement or suggestions that make the task easier, but the adult should not give the answer or complete the task. If the adult does the latter, children may think the adult doesn't believe they are capable of doing it themselves. Repeating this mistake can further convince children they are not capable. Peer teaching (pairing a more capable student with a struggling student) can be beneficial to both children. But it is important to train the helper to assist—not to complete the activity for the struggling child. Doing it for the child is not helping them at all.

Sense of Capability

Children's sense of capability is another factor that affects their confidence. Children need to feel they can do things for themselves. This is especially true at ages two and three, when you hear "I do it myself" constantly. But even older children, who may try to get adults to give them an answer to a math problem or spell a word for them, would rather do tasks themselves. Doing things independently really feels good.

Some children are quick learners or have obvious talents. But even those children need time and opportunity to practice a skill before they succeed at it. Take time to help children practice and concentrate on the effort just as much as the result. Make sure you understand the child's definition of success at this skill, because often a child's measure of success differs from an adult's.

When you are helping children develop skills, consider two key questions: Do they have the large-muscle and small-muscle coordination to master the skill? Do they have the cognitive ability to master the skill? Consider the task of tying shoelaces. Some children learn it in a day, while others take months before they can get it right. If children do not have the large- and small-muscle development they need, they will be unable to tie shoelaces no matter how many times you show them or how many times they try. So your role in this situation is to plan activities that help children develop their small muscles, such as stringing beads, picking up cotton balls with tweezers, or using lacing cards. Playing bend-and-stretch or marching like soldiers will help develop the large muscles. Achieving a sense of capability requires a combination of timing, development, desire, and repetition.

Feeling Loved

Feeling loved is essential for children to develop confidence. Unconditional love gives children a sense of intrinsic self-worth. When love is unconditional, it is given freely, without reservation, and without expectation of anything in return. Unconditional love is given even when the relationship is not great—even if the receiver made a mistake or told a lie.

Adults can show that they love and value children by understanding that all children have different learning needs and by helping children learn at their own pace. Choosing activities related to children's interests helps them feel understood. Establishing an atmosphere in which children are accepted for who they are, including not only their abilities but also their personal failings, makes the children feel loved unconditionally. Calling children by name or commenting on their projects can help children feel important and appreciated. Remembering something that children said they were going to do and asking them about it later sends a message that they matter. When children do something—successfully or not—that you want them to repeat, give them sincere recognition for their effort. This positive recognition will make them feel competent and confident to try again.

Children feel unloved when they do not feel safe. So create a place where children feel safe and all children are treated equally. This environment demonstrates love for all to see.

Children are going to make mistakes—even ones that adults feel should not happen because they have explained their rules and expectations repeatedly.

Each mistake children make can become a learning moment or a blow to a child's self-worth. It is not the mistake, but what you do after the mistake that is the most important. When an adult gets upset or frustrated, children can sense that and may withdraw from that person. The emotional state of the adult dictates the child's emotional state. Often it is a good idea to take a few minutes to breathe and calm yourself. Once you are calm, you can help the child generate other solutions to use when faced with this problem again. Your example helps the child see that calming oneself is a good first step to finding alternate solutions. While you are calmly addressing the issue, encourage the child to participate in the solution process rather than withdraw from it.

Allowing children to speak and listening to what they say helps them feel respected. Help children feel good about themselves and love who they are and who they are becoming. Loving themselves for who they are is truly a gift.

Sense of Acceptance

Humans are social by nature. Acceptance by a peer group is integral to a person's confidence. Children thrive when people accept them for who they are. They need to feel a sense of belonging in their home, school, child care, and community.

The way you interact with children tells them a lot about how you feel about them. Most children crave affection, such as hugging or holding hands. To children, affection indicates acceptance. Tone of voice and body language say a lot too. Smiling at children sends the message that you like them, while frowning tells children you are disappointed in them and do not accept them. Consistent treatment of children is essential in creating a sense of acceptance. When you show favoritism to some children, other children get the message that they are somehow lacking and not acceptable to you.

In addition to feeling acceptance from others, children need to accept themselves for who they are. Children learn to accept themselves when their strengths are celebrated. Create an accepting environment where all children feel valued, regardless of their strengths or shortcomings. Give children opportunities to identify what they are good at, what they like to do, and what they do not like to do. You can begin by making a list of what each child likes to do and what they would like to do better. Schoolagers can do this independently, while preschoolers will need an adult to write their list for them, as in the following vignette.

At a small rural preschool, during group time the teacher introduced a new area he called an *interview station*. He showed the children a piece of paper that had three sections. The sections were labeled "I like to do," "What I want to learn to do," and "What I do not like to do." Over the next few days, the children met individually with the teacher to fill out their interviews. He wrote down their answers. He encouraged the children to draw pictures that described their answers.

The teacher reviewed each paper. The interviews provided lots of information he could use for planning the environment and future activities. He used this information to create spaces that correlated with what the children liked to do and wanted to learn. The interviews also told him how the children felt about their own abilities, helped him understand if children had a fixed mind-set or a growth mind-set, and gave him information about who needed what kind of support. Armed with this information, he was able to create a physical environment that reflected the children's interests while providing a responsive emotional environment with opportunities for all children to succeed.

PROVIDERS' ROLE

Intentional Teaching

Confidence begins with children's perception that they can do a given task, so teaching children confidence begins with understanding how children feel about their own abilities. Even if you think a child is good at something, that does not mean the child thinks so. Determine which children believe in their ability to succeed with hard work. Work with children to encourage perseverance and resilience. Help children see that they can recover from disappointment and improve their skills if they continue to work hard.

Encourage children to figure out how they can help others rather than hurt them. Provide opportunities for children to identify their skills and talents as well as the skills and talents of their peers. Help children set realistic goals. Realistic goals can be different for children of the same age, so know what each child can do and set goals that are achievable for that child. Use one-on-one time to engage children in conversations about how they have improved over time. Help them remember when they couldn't do something and how practice helped them be able to do it now. Provide genuine recognition for a job well done or a skill that has improved. Children need training, support, and encouragement when they are trying new things. Include ways for children to lead their peers in a game or to mentor younger children.

Design the environment to meet the needs of all the children in care. Examine the materials and supplies within the program space to make sure that they are age and skill level appropriate. Make sure that you have a variety of materials and games that children can easily complete and others that might challenge the children, to expand their knowledge or skill level.

Respect children for who they are. Plan activities around what children enjoy. Learn about the children's culture. Work toward including some of their customs in your program planning.

Environment Design

Environmental Elements That Foster Confidence

PHYSICAL ENVIRONMENT	TEMPORAL ENVIRONMENT	INTERPERSONAL ENVIRONMENT
• Variety of activities that span the range of abilities of children	• Opportunities for cooperative play and project activities	• Clear expectations for children's jobs to set children up for success
• Puzzles with a variety of numbers of pieces	• Opportunities to lead a game by giving directions to other children	• Opportunities to take on a leadership role
• Books that span from picture books to chapter books	• Meaningful, age-appropriate jobs for children	• Opportunities to watch before entering an activity
• Board games at different skill levels, such as Candy Land, Chutes and Ladders, checkers, and chess	• Time to practice routines, such as lining up, washing hands, and what to do at mealtime	• Mentoring program in which older children help younger children
• Variety of card games, such as Go Fish and UNO		

Strategies for Intentional Teaching and Encouraging Skill Development

- Help children set realistic, attainable goals.
- Plan with children's skills in mind.
- Encourage children to use positive self-talk when they feel frustrated.
- Help children become bucket fillers.
- Create opportunities for children to help others.
- Choose activities that reflect the children's interests.
- Create activities that encourage children to self-identify their own areas of strength.
- Create activities that encourage children to identify areas of strength in others.

PARENT AND STAFF EDUCATION STRATEGIES

People often believe that others judge them the same way they judge themselves. But this is seldom true; people often judge themselves more harshly than others do. Have your program's staff members assess themselves, determining what they are good at and what they are not. Then have the staff say what they like or admire about their coworkers. This activity can help adults validate one another's skills and improve their own self-image. Once staff members do this activity, they can do it with children. The staff will have a better idea about the emotions children might experience when assessing themselves, and the adults will be able to provide appropriate support in the process.

Just like children, adults need to feel accepted and valued. Find ways to recognize staff members for a job well done, and encourage them to do the same for the children in their care. Assess their areas of strength, and find tasks that will utilize their strengths. Give the staff training, feedback, and support when they are taking on a new task or role within the program. Communicate tips to staff and family members for how to create or increase confidence in children. Communicate when children have made strides in achieving a personal goal. Help adults understand the benefits of validating a child's abilities and the emotions associated with not being able to complete something. With this understanding, adults can help children learn how to bounce back from failure and disappointment.

Things to Remember

- Not all children have the same abilities.
- Children will not always be successful.
- Children need to feel that they *can* be successful.
- Help children achieve a growth mind-set.
- Concentrate on and encourage children's efforts.
- Give sincere, truthful compliments.
- Self-image develops over time.
- Feeling loved can help children develop a positive self-image.
- Children need to feel safe.

Children's Books Dealing with Confidence

- *The Girl Who Never Made Mistakes* by Mark Pett and Gary Rubinstein
- *I Can Handle It!* by Laurie Wright
- *I Matter* by Laurie Wright
- *In My Heart* by Jo Witek
- *Incredible You!* by Wayne W. Dyer
- *The Invisible Boy* by Trudy Ludwig
- *The Most Magnificent Thing* by Ashley Spires
- *You Are Special* by Max Lucado
- *Your Fantastic Elastic Brain* by JoAnn Deak

CHAPTER 7

Curiosity

WHAT IS CURIOSITY?

Curiosity is a desire to learn about things, people, and ideas. This interest leads to inquiry. Curiosity sparks children's love of adventure and their need to play.

Children are born curious. Think of how long and how intently infants will look at a toy, move it from hand to hand, or stick it in their mouths. When infants do this, they are trying to figure out the toy. Is it soft or hard? Does it taste good? Does food come out of it? What noise does it make? Toddlers may take wooden beads and repeatedly put them in a cup and pour them out. When toddlers do this, they are exploring volume. Do all the beads fit into the cup each time? Do the beads fit better if they put all the red ones in first? You may find that young children will play with the same toy or materials for a long time and then move to another activity, only to return to the first activity the next day. Children need time to digest what they have learned during play. Once they have learned something, they may return to the activity where they learned it to test their new knowledge. In most cases, young children engage in this type of curiosity without communicating what they are trying to learn or have learned.

Children may smile or clap when they succeed or may cry or walk away when they are frustrated. When young children show frustration, this is the time for adults to step in and help them become successful. Adults might sit next to children and play with them, following their lead. Once a child has succeeded, adults can back out of the play but stay close and be available for help if needed.

All play starts with children acting out what they see, such as cooking in the kitchen, taking care of a younger sibling, or gardening. Play then expands from children's experiences to children's imagination. Use open-ended materials to stimulate imagination.

Open-ended materials have no prescribed use or expected outcome; they can be used in many ways. With open-ended materials, children are the orchestrators of play. As play researcher Walter F. Drew (2007) explains, "There are no expectations, no specific problems to solve, no rules to follow, and no pressure to produce a finished product. It's all about free play—the freedom to invent and discover." Open-ended materials can be used by children of different ages. Children of different ages interact with the same open-ended material in different ways. Open-ended materials include (among many other items) blocks, sand and water tables, playdough, paints, art supplies, generic dolls, cars, animal figures, glitter, yarn, cotton balls, foam shapes, stickers, rubber stamps, bingo dabbers, and fabric scraps. When presented with open-ended materials, children become curious about them and use their imagination to make things and dream up scenarios. For example, children might use blocks to make a truck, train, or tall building. They might add people, animals, or cars to extend the block play. They might build a house for the people, put people or animals on a train or in the building, or build a garage for the cars.

By contrast, single-purpose or closed-ended materials have limited uses. They have rules or a predetermined outcome or a right answer, or they don't allow for individual differences (Frost et al. 2004). Some examples of closed-ended materials are puzzles and board games. According to Mr. Rogers, the author of *The Mr. Rogers Parenting Resource Book*, "The very best kinds of playthings are open-ended. . . . Children can make of them whatever they're working on at that moment, and their play is then determined by their own needs. If most of their playthings are 'single-action' toys, their play tends to be limited, as if they're following the 'formula' of what the manufacturer determined" (Li and Robb 2015).

Modern media programming and products can profoundly influence the ways in which children play. Today's children are bombarded with images on television, online, and in digital apps, as well as with media-linked closed-ended toys. When children get a lot of exposure to such media and materials, it may constrict their play to reenacting the same media-linked stories over and over. Their play may become an imitation of what they see rather than an imaginative and creative expansion on their real-life experience and observation. Media-linked toys seldom take on attributes other than those their official characters possess. For example, a toy version of a princess character seldom becomes a doctor or a mom, and a toy version of a superhero character typically does not mow the lawn or become a dad. For this reason, it's wise to limit children's exposure to media and closed-ended toys to a few times a week, and encourage new story lines for the favorite toys. This approach allows children more time and opportunity for curiosity and creativity.

Curiosity needs to be nurtured in order to grow. Adults may not know how or when to nurture children's curiosity. Often adults lead children into their own adult way of thinking about a certain thing or event, rather than allowing children to investigate on their own. If adults don't like messy materials, such as finger paint, playdough, sand, and water, adults may not offer these activities to children. Some adults may feel that they have to plan every minute of children's awake time. They may worry that if children don't have a full schedule, they will get bored or get into trouble. But children need downtime. Unscheduled time allows children to learn how to relax, regenerate, take up a hobby, explore, get outdoors and enjoy nature, or simply be bored. Boredom is a springboard to curiosity. When children have free time and opportunities for unstructured play, they tend to explore. To create exploration opportunities, adults can start by determining what the children are interested in and offering materials and activities to expand children's thinking. Linking materials and play opportunities to your lesson plans helps children work through what they know and what they do not understand. Making these opportunities as independent as possible allows children to learn at their own speed. Give them time to investigate and become curious about how something works or develop a desire to learn a new way to do something. Some children will do something once and understand it and move on, while others will need time to try, test, observe, and retest.

During a site visit, a teacher explained that she was having a hard time with a child misusing glue. She explained that every day this child poured copious amounts of glue on paper, then dragged yarn through the puddle of glue. After dragging the yarn back and forth, the child pulled the dripping yarn through her fingers, creating a mess all over herself and the table. The teacher clearly did not like the mess or what she saw as a misuse of glue.

I asked the teacher, "Why do you think the child is repeatedly coming to the art area and playing with the glue?"

The teacher said, "I do not know, but this has to stop. That glue costs a lot of money, and it is just a mess. The gluey yarn balls roll all over the floor."

I sat down with the child at the art area. I asked the child what she liked about the glue. She said, "It is fun and smooth and cold and sticky."

I asked the teacher, "What do you think the child is trying to tell you she wants to learn about?" The teacher was perplexed, so I shared the child's answer to my question regarding what she liked about the glue. I emphasized the child's wonderfully descriptive words.

The teacher said, "She's trying to understand how glue works. So how do we get her to stop?"

I explained, "The child will not stop unless you remove all glue from the art area. But that would send the message that exploration is not a good thing."

I encouraged the teacher to place balls of fiber, such as yarn of different colors, weights, and textures, cotton and nylon string, and sisal twine in small plastic containers with an X cut into each lid, so that the end of the fiber could be pulled through the X. This strategy would allow the child to use the balls of fiber without them rolling all over the glue and the floor. I also suggested covering the art table with a plastic tablecloth.

The child—and soon the other children too—began to experiment with the variety of fibers and began creating pictures on paper with their gluey string, yarn, and twine. In about a week, the experimentation was complete, and the children were no longer interested in the glue and string. Before switching out the materials, the teacher debriefed with the children during group time, asking the following questions:

- Which type of string did you like best?
- Which string was the softest?
- Which string stuck to the paper the easiest?
- Which was the hardest to stick?
- What are some words that describe the glue?

Even though the teacher was frustrated at first, she allowed the glue-and-string discovery to continue. She modified the space to make cleanup easier, thus reducing her stress. She followed the child's lead and allowed the child the time and freedom to test, draw some conclusions, readjust the process, retest, and record her findings. This is the basis of scientific inquiry and creativity.

According to Kathryn Starke (2012), literacy specialist and founder of Creative Minds Publications, "Creativity isn't formally assessed or evaluated on tests or report cards, so teachers rarely plan lessons that encourage it." Many people believe that creativity occurs only in the arts. I disagree. Creativity is the process of thinking originally and trying new and unique ways to make something happen that may not have existed before. Creativity can occur in any endeavor. Adults encourage creativity when they provide time, protected space, open-ended materials, and opportunities for imaginative play and exploration.

Children explore materials in different ways as they grow. For example, when young children begin building with blocks, they may be able to build a tower with only three blocks. The desire to make a bigger tower—maybe as big as or bigger than those of other children—leads to exploration, testing, and experimentation, during which children learn what is needed to complete a taller tower. By trial and error, children work until they achieve their goal, learning about balance, support, and alignment along the way.

When you are planning your program environment, be sure to plan spaces that encourage imaginative play. Equipping designated spaces with materials that generate open-ended play is the foundation for creativity. For example, a dramatic play space equipped with materials for rotating themes allows children to interact safely in different settings and work through ideas and scenarios that arise within them. Some popular dramatic play space themes are as follows:

- ordinary home
- airport
- campsite
- castle
- flower shop
- grocery store
- pizza parlor or other restaurant
- newspaper office
- music store
- beach at the ocean
- business office

- pet shop
- shoe store
- theater
- veterinarian's office

Take time to create theme boxes that contain books, materials, props, and supplies to support each theme. Allow children's input into what should be placed within these theme boxes to create buy in and encourage exploration. Keep an inventory sheet for each box so you can replace or track down items that have been used up or misplaced. For an example of a theme box inventory sheet, see appendix D. Link dramatic play spaces to weekly or monthly curriculum themes. If possible, plan an outing to help the children further explore and understand what they are learning. Assigning roles and acting out familiar situations or reenacting things that they have seen on an outing can be a great way for children to understand relationships and real-world situations. It is amazing what children can do with a box of dress-up clothes and a few props.

ASSOCIATED SKILLS

Adventurousness

Being adventurous comes naturally to some people. Children who possess a fearless temperament will dive into an activity and take chances, assuming that they have everything under control and that everything will turn out fine in the end. But not all children have the temperament for adventure. Children with a fearful temperament may be reluctant to try anything new. Adults need to intentionally plan with fearful children in mind by providing ways for all children to participate in an activity. For example, preschoolers can help the teacher determine what materials are needed in the art area or help choose puzzles for the game table. Schoolagers could take notes for planning what will need to go in the dramatic play area for a specific theme, or take notes about how a science project was conducted. Working in pairs can help fearful children try an activity. Children may be more willing to take risks when they do not have to do something alone.

Adults spend a vast amount of time planning interesting and fun things for children, only to become upset when the children do not engage in the activities. To avoid this frustration, ask the children what they are interested in and would like to know more about. When children are involved in planning, they can direct exploration toward things that are interesting to them. During group time, ask the children to generate a list of things they already know about. Write the topics on chart paper. Ask the children to choose one topic from the list that they would like to know more about. Write the topic at the top of a new piece of chart paper, then draw three columns below. At the top of the first column, write a *K*, ask the children what they already *know* about the topic, and chart their answers. At the top of the second column, write a *W*, ask the children what they *wonder* about the topic, and chart their answers. Use the information in the *K* and *W* columns to plan upcoming lessons and design learning spaces and activities. Once the children have exhausted the topic, it is time to change the theme. But before you make the switch, return to the chart paper and fill in the final column. At the top of the third column, write an *L*, ask the children what they have *learned* about the topic, and chart their answers. To choose a new theme, refer back to the first list the children generated (things they already know about) and ask the children which topic they would like to explore. If some or all of the topics are no longer interesting to the children, ask them if they would like to add any new topics to the list.

The KWL approach to planning is a win-win for adults and children. It helps the teacher plan activities and environments that will increase children's engagement and learning. When children articulate what they have learned, they cement the knowledge they've gained. Sharing control with children allows them to have some power over their learning experiences.

One teacher used the KWL approach to generate themes for her lesson plans. Using the list of things the children wondered about, she found that four topics dovetailed nicely together, so she planned accordingly. Her first theme was rockets. She turned the dramatic play space into command central. In the art area, the children could design rockets. In the science area, children could make rockets with two drinking straws. She set up a launchpad in the group meeting area, where children could test their straw rockets and then revise them and retry them, marking their rockets' distance traveled with their names written on sticky labels. When it was time to change the theme, the teacher transitioned to a theme on space and planets. She added pretend moondust (a mixture of dry coffee grounds, cornstarch, and sand) to the sensory area.

The sensory area also offered children a variety of balls of varied weights. The children could drop different balls into the moondust, creating different-size craters. The children compared the sizes and depths of the craters. After the children exhausted this theme, the teacher continued with a theme of day and night and a theme of light and shadows.

In this story, the teacher not only used a KWL approach to plan lessons, but also looked for common threads that arose in the topics to help her move smoothly from one theme to another. While many programs define the amount of time to be spent on each lesson plan, it is best to take your timing cues from the children. Inevitably, if you think the interest in a specific theme will be two weeks, either the children are done in a week or less, or the interest lasts for a month. Remember that children process information and ideas at different paces, so not all children will finish a theme at the same time or gather the same information from the process.

Excite children by creating opportunities to learn about things they are interested in. Provide time for children to explore a theme from many angles. Stoke the desire to learn by providing a variety of children's activities, books, magazines, and colorful posters on the topic and by using a variety of learning formats, such as art, science, and small- and large-group activities. Bring in speakers, and consult related organizations for additional resources and activity-planning ideas.

De-stressing

When children are stressed, their energies are diverted to crisis management, and they are unable to be curious about anything. Stress in children has many causes, including family strife, bullying, constant testing in school to determine where children are cognitively and socially, and pressure from caring adults to be the best at everything. Stress in children can manifest through increased worry, sadness, irritability, and withdrawal. Most children cannot hide these signs of stress, so they should be easy to spot as children interact with adults, peers, and their environment.

To reduce stress, adults need to help children identify when they are stressed and what caused the stress. Children need to understand that they cannot control causes of stress, but they can use de-stressing strategies when they spot a stress inducer in daily life or when their stress level begins to rise. De-stressing is the process of releasing stress.

There are many ways to de-stress. Most children have robust imaginations, so they can easily visualize an activity in a place that makes them feel calm, such as playing in the sand at a beach, swinging on a backyard swing, or fishing with a grandparent. Such visualization helps children regain control of their thoughts and emotions. Total body relaxation is another way to drain away stress. Children can purposefully tighten and relax individual muscles, starting at the head and working all the way down the body to the toes. This de-stressing strategy works well for children who need a concrete physical activity to manage stress. Another strategy is controlled breathing. A technique called belly breathing, often used for children with asthma, is a great stress reducer. Children begin by placing their hand on their stomach. They breathe in through their nose until they can take in no more air. They will be able to feel the incoming air, as their belly will rise. Then they will slowly blow out through their mouths (like blowing out a candle) to a count of ten. After repeating this process five to ten times, children can feel the stress melt away. Regular physical exercise is another effective way to reduce stress. Planning time to integrate these stress-relieving strategies can help minimize children's stress as well as their disruptive behaviors. Once children can identify stress and use de-stressing strategies, they can move from crisis to investigation. Visualization, total body relaxation, and controlled breathing before naptime or bedtime, after school, during group time, or before a visit from a guest speaker can help the children relax so that they can be calm and focused on the task at hand. Offer weekly exercise video sessions as a choice along with going outdoors or on days with inclement weather.

Keep in mind that a predictable schedule allows children to know what will happen next and that knowledge is important in reducing stress. Adults do not like to have their schedules disrupted or changed without notice, and children are no different. When children are not worried about what is happening next, they can become engaged in the planned activities and spaces within the program environment. Consider posting a schedule on the wall with an arrow attached, and move the arrow down the chart as the children change from one activity to the next. This chart can help the children manage their day while reducing stress caused by not knowing what comes next. If the day will be disrupted by a speaker or field trip, or if an unforeseen event occurs, tell the children at the beginning of their day or as soon as possible, and remind them about the change before it occurs. These strategies are easy to implement and can help create a peaceful classroom.

Also, remember that downtime is the key to reducing stress in children. Downtime allows the mind to wander and ponder. It provides a respite from the pressures of daily routines and time to relax and regroup. Ultimately, downtime is the pathway to curiosity.

Exploring

Exploring is the willingness to discover possibilities. It is finding the wonder in everyday things. It is being able to look at something and see it not only for what it is, but also for what it could be. Explorers take the time to investigate and learn for themselves the many facets of an item, idea, or situation. An explorer looks at problems and figures out new ways to solve them.

Creating explorers requires time, resources, encouragement, and acceptance of alternate explanations and ideas. Children need time to immerse themselves into investigation and time to connect the dots between what they previously thought and what they are learning. Exploration without a timeline or an expected outcome allows children to determine what they want to know and allows them to experiment with how to find out that information. Sometimes children will start exploring one idea and that leads them to another interest. While the connection may be clear in their minds, it may make no sense to adults. "Why" questions are the signal of explorers wanting to understand. "Why does the dog lose its hair?" "Why can't I see the stars during the day?" "Why does the moon change shapes?" For adults, the easy response is simply to answer the children's questions. But a simple answer thwarts the learning process. Instead, adults should capitalize on children's inquiry and encourage exploration.

To encourage exploration, adults can provide activities that enable children to see how things work. For example, place a toaster or radio (with the cord removed) in a "take-apart" space. Let children disassemble the item and place like parts together. The children can then use these parts to create other objects or artworks. Keep the children safe during this exploration by providing goggles, aprons, and child-size screwdrivers and Allen wrenches. Cover the worktable with a nonskid mat to prevent slipping and dropping. Create a scavenger hunt outdoors by taking pictures of things you would like the children to find or learn about. Encourage young children to use the pictures provided to find the desired items. Children can use photos or drawn pictures to create their own scavenger hunts to be shared with other children. Challenge older children to photograph or draw pictures of only a part of each item, and ask the children to write down what item that part belongs to. Another exploration idea is the tell-me-about-it game. Provide a picture or the name of an item, and challenge the children to find the item and tell you as much as they can about it. Encourage them to measure it, tell its location, describe what its use might be, explain how it feels, describe its color, and so on. Activities like these place children in the role of explorer and help them develop inquiry, research, and documentation skills while fueling their imaginations.

PROVIDERS' ROLE

Intentional Teaching

When children are relaxed and calm, they are better able to engage in learning and exploration. Children need to learn how to reduce stress and recenter themselves so they can get involved in the task at hand, so adults need to intentionally teach children stress-relieving activities and provide calming spaces. Include soft areas within the environment as a space where children can relax. Also include other spaces and activities that tend to reduce stress. For example, at a sensory table, children can experience a variety of sensory materials, such as sand, water, snow, dirt, foam peanuts, bubbles, and so on. Children should have access to a place where they can run and play daily, both indoors and out. Create quiet places that allow children to listen to music or write in their journals, draw pictures that describe their feelings, create a story, or remake a familiar story. Create a daily schedule that helps children know what is coming next, and remind them of any changes to their typical day.

Maintain an attitude of and include activities and events for encouraging exploration, investigation and adventure. Be deliberate when developing lesson plans, and outline the activities you will be providing in a given day or week. Make sure that the lesson plan reflects themes and topics in which the children are interested. Add interest to familiar themes. Just because it is fall and you are talking about trees and leaves for the umpteenth time does not mean you cannot encourage creativity and spark curiosity. For example, something as simple as asking why some leaves are yellow and others are red can cause children to wonder. Chart the children's answers to your question, research the topic, and then teach them why leaves change color in the fall and why they turn different colors.

How you introduce a new area or activity is important to engaging the children. If you are excited about it, chances are the children will be excited too. Conversely, if you are just going through the motions, then the children may respond similarly. If you have worked hard on an area or an activity and the children do not seem interested in it, ask yourself the following questions:

- Where did the idea for the area or activity come from—staff or children? Creating an activity that centers on what the children like to do may persuade children to visit that area.
- Is the area inviting? Kneel within the area and observe it from the children's vantage point. Cool colors such as blues and greens can calm the children and should be used in quiet and rest areas. Warm tones of yellow and brown can aide in concentration and are appropriate for homework and collaborative learning spaces. Other warm tones, such as red and orange, can energize and stimulate appetite and work well in large active spaces and eating areas. Matching the colors used in a space with the purpose of the space can help achieve the purpose of the space.
- Are children unsure how to use a new space or new materials, or how to do a new activity? Announcing a new space alerts children that it exists. When you introduce new materials, new activities, or new spaces, use group time to show and explain what is new and how to use it.
- Do the children have all the materials they need to be successful in an area? Replenish materials as they get used up.
- Can children reach everything they need? Provide materials that are accessible to all children.
- Is it clear how many children can occupy a center at once? Provide a visual representation of how many children can play within the center by using place mats, chairs, or a sign at the entrance showing the maximum occupancy.

Provide free-choice time, during which children can choose whom and what to play with and where to play. Provide a balance of active and quiet areas. Provide places and opportunities that cause children to think outside the box and resources to expand their thinking on a given topic. Look at ways for children to explore the familiar as well as ideas that challenge children's thinking. Encourage diverse opinions and ideas.

Environment Design

Environmental Elements That Foster Curiosity

PHYSICAL ENVIRONMENT	TEMPORAL ENVIRONMENT	INTERPERSONAL ENVIRONMENT
• Resources that help promote new ways of thinking	• Sustained periods of time for imaginative play	• Peer sharing and teaching
• Science experiences that engage children and allow for exploration	• Resources that stimulate higher-level thinking and problem solving	• Group activities
• Retelling familiar stories with different endings and characters	• Project work that allows the children to reflect, revise, and retry	• Supporting and encouraging children's imagination through play
• Open-ended materials	• Scavenger hunts to encourage exploration, documentation, and scientific inquiry	• Providing materials that encourage children to think outside the box and engage children in the creative process
• Examples of abstract art and free-form sculptures		• Avoiding the attitude that there is only one way to make or do something
• Displays of children's creative art projects		• Letting children take the lead; facilitating play instead of directing it
• Games with rules that are created by the children		
• A place where children can put creations so they can be finished at a later date		

Strategies for Intentional Teaching and Encouraging Skill Development

- Provide opportunities that allow children to think outside the box.
- Encourage and celebrate curiosity and creativity.
- Make available a large variety of art supplies and ample time for children to create open-ended art projects using a variety of media.

Provide materials such as tempera paint, watercolors, markers, crayons, chalk, modeling clay, playdough, wood, wire, and papier-mâché to allow for free-form artwork.

- Provide science experiments for children to test and retest.
- Encourage children to ask questions.
- Provide resources to help children make sense of the world around them.

PARENT AND STAFF EDUCATION STRATEGIES

Teach staff that creativity is messy, and that it is more about the process of curiosity that fuels exploration than it is about the end product. Provide professional development that helps adults understand the creative process. At staff meetings, encourage creativity and provide hands-on activities to help staff realize firsthand the benefits of doing these types of activities with children. Hire staff who understand the creative process, provide appropriate materials, embrace the mess, and encourage exploration.

Help parents understand that children learn through play. Help families understand the creative process and offer suggestions about what they could do at home to encourage creativity. Publish these tips, activities, and strategies through written and electronic media. Engage families in the creative process by asking for materials and supplies that will enhance children's exploration and discovery during their time in your program. Share with parents what themes you are planning and what learning is taking place, so parents can support what is being taught in the classroom at home. Share tips about how the family can extend learning at home by posting tips in the classroom, sharing them in a newsletter, or posting them on a parent bulletin board.

Invite community artists and inventors into the program. Host a creative night with families to showcase their children's projects. Encourage parents to participate in designing activities with staff to better understand the benefits of these projects. Invite local media to cover the creative night. Or, write a story and take photos to submit to your local newspaper and place on your program's website.

Things to Remember

- Curiosity is key to children's engagement.
- Through curiosity, children learn about the world around them.

- Unfettered play sparks curiosity.
- Creativity does not occur just in art.
- Embrace children's "why" questions.
- Encourage new ideas.
- Plan for exploration.
- If the adult is excited about exploration and discovery, the children will be too.
- Stress blocks creativity.
- Integrate de-stressing activities within the daily schedule so children can be free to concentrate on play.
- Post a daily schedule so children know what to expect next, reducing stress and increasing their ability to be creative and curious.
- Use lesson plan themes to scaffold knowledge by bridging prior knowledge to new experiences.

Children's Books Dealing with Curiosity

- *Beautiful Oops!* by Barney Saltzberg
- *Bored No More* by Jen Burns
- *Chalk* by Bill Thomson
- *The Day the Crayons Quit* by Drew Daywalt
- *The Dot* by Peter H. Reynolds
- *Going Places* by Peter Reynolds and Paul Reynolds
- *Iggy Peck, Architect* by Andrea Beaty
- *Magic Box* by Katie Cleminson
- *Pandora the Curious* by Joan Holub and Suzanne Williams
- *Roxaboxen* by Alice McLerran
- *Weslandia* by Paul Fleischman
- *What Do You Do with an Idea?* by Kobi Yamada
- *Wild Dragon Soul* by Tatjana Garibaldi

CHAPTER 8

Control

WHAT IS CONTROL?

Control is the ability to regulate one's actions and redirect inappropriate behaviors. Self-control is a process of getting oneself under control if presented with a difficult situation or the inability to get one's needs met. According to research published in the journal *PNAS*, "Self-control is an umbrella construct that bridges concepts and measurements from different disciplines (e.g., impulsivity, conscientiousness, self-regulation, delay of gratification, and inattention-hyperactivity, executive function, willpower, intertemporal choice)" (Moffitt et al. 2011).

When people exercise self-control, they do not act on feelings alone. They take time to think of the consequences of an action before choosing to do it. For instance, let's say a child gets pushed when lining up to go outdoors. If the child has self-control skills, they can consider what will result from pushing the pusher back. The teacher might notice and send the child indoors or to the back of the line. Or the child could just move away and give the pusher plenty of room, then go outdoors to play. The better choice may seem obvious, but if a child does not have control skills, they may use emotion instead of logic to deal with this situation.

Teaching children to manage their feelings can eliminate negative behaviors, such as pushing, hitting, biting, and tantrums. Eating a balanced and nutritious diet, having a regular schedule, and getting enough sleep can go a long way toward reducing emotion-driven behavior. Children do not cope well with inconsistent schedules, disturbed sleep, or poor nutrition. According to the Division of Sleep Medicine (DSM) at Harvard Medical School, poor or inadequate sleep habits can cause irritability, anxiety, stress, and an increase in negative emotions, such as anger and sadness (2008).

Children who cannot control their behavior when they are dealing with strong emotions, such as anger, sadness, and frustration, can pose problems for themselves and their peers. Children without control make impulsive decisions. They act without considering the consequences, which are often negative. By contrast, young children who develop good self-control skills have "reductions in teen pregnancy, school dropout, delinquency, and work absenteeism" later in life. In addition, research has shown that childhood self-control positively affects one's overall health in adulthood. Young children with poor self-control tend to have increased debt and financial instability later in life (Moffitt et al. 2011).

Children who act out may do so because they do not feel like anyone is hearing them. They may want or need something, but they know only one way to get what they desire. Frequently, children just need adults to listen. A care provider in a room full of young children may find it hard to listen to one child without hearing everything else going on in the room or thinking of all the other things that need to be done. When you find yourself in a situation like this, remember that time taken now to focus on the child may prevent an incident later. It also conveys to the child that you value what he or she has to say. Try taking a few deep breaths before you begin the conversation. This action can clear your head and help you focus on the child before you. Getting down on the child's eye level or holding the child's hand can also help you focus. Give the child time to talk without interruption. Children often have a hard time putting into words what they want to say or how they are feeling, so it's important to listen patiently. The more hurried a child feels an adult is, the more apt the child is to fumble over words, not make sense, or tell the story out of sequence. If the child seems flustered, encourage them to slow down, take a few breaths, and start over from the beginning. Stop whatever else you are doing to make sure the child knows you have time for the conversation. Once they have finished, recap the story and try to identify the child's emotion to make sure you understand both the feelings and the events of the story. Once you understand the story and emotion, ask the child how they responded to the situation in the story, and talk about other possible ways to react to that situation, to provide tools for future situations. This can be a time-consuming process. Changes will not happen overnight.

When a child wants control of a situation, a power struggle between the child and an adult can occur. Avoiding a power struggle whenever possible is important. When adults are able to control their emotions while dealing with tough situations, they show children how to do the same. Adults demonstrate strategies and words that can help children manage future challenges, as in the following example.

A child was in a preschool room with fourteen other children. She was swinging around a large, flat board from the block area. Rather than get into a power struggle, the teacher called the child by name and told her that it was unsafe to swing the board around. The teacher asked the child where the board belonged. The child said the board belonged in the block area. The teacher asked her to put it back into that area. She put it back into the block area and went to another activity without incident.

In this scenario, the teacher gave the child specific reasons why she could not swing the board around and explained exactly what the child should do with the board. By telling the child exactly what she needed to do, the teacher left no doubt about what was expected. This approach allowed the child to make an appropriate decision and provided an opportunity for a positive outcome. If the teacher had chosen to take the board away from the child or had yelled, "Put that away," a power struggle could have ensued, causing the child to stand her ground and hold on to the board for dear life. This approach would not have given the child any reason to stop swinging the board, nor would it outline what the child *should* do with the board. By telling the child where to put the board, the teacher eliminated the chance that the child might not choose the same place the teacher was thinking of. A physical injury could have occurred if the child chose to run with the board or throw it to the ground.

When you tell children what you want them to do rather than what you do not want them to do, you help children make acceptable choices. You might think, "They have been in this room for months; they should know better." But children forget, just as adults do. Think about all the times you couldn't recall what someone told you, what you had for lunch yesterday, or how a policy was worded. Children who pass through multiple rule-based environments each day have a hard time switching gears and remembering what they can or should do in each environment or with each adult. Children have much less life experience to draw on and much less experience at gear switching than adults have. Adults cannot expect children to remember everything—especially things they may not even understand. What is more, it is developmentally normal for young children to be self-focused. If children believe that a rule doesn't benefit them, then they may see no point in following it.

Breaking down instructions into manageable parts and telling children exactly what you want them to do will help them be successful and reduce your stress.

> Sharlyn was playing with two other children. The teacher said it was time to clean up for lunch. Sharlyn started throwing toys and yelling. The teacher went up to Sharlyn, got down on the child's eye level, and said, "You seem mad about cleaning up."
>
> Sharlyn replied, "Yes."
>
> "Is there something you would like to leave out so you can play with it again after lunch?" said the teacher.
>
> Sharlyn responded, "No." Then she picked up a toy and wound up to throw it.
>
> The teacher took the toy from Sharlyn and explained, "It is not safe to throw toys because we might hurt our friends."
>
> Sharlyn said, "I don't care."
>
> The teacher said, "I think we need to take a walk to calm down so we can safely rejoin our friends." The teacher walked Sharlyn around the center, talking to her about why she was so mad. When Sharlyn said she was ready, they went back into the classroom. Sharlyn went to her table for lunch and began chatting with the children at her table.

When children are having a hard time getting themselves under control, removing them from the class (if staffing allows) is a great way to have a private conversation. This does not mean sending them to the office or another room. It means providing an adult-directed option to calm down, such as a walk around the center or around the block together while holding hands. Holding hands while children calm down shows them you are there and are willing to talk when they are ready. Adults can help angry children reset their emotions by chatting about unrelated things they did in class or by pointing out interesting sights on the walk. Once children are calm, it is time to talk about the problem behavior. Start the conversation by asking, "Are you ready to talk about why you were so mad when _____?" You may need to prompt them by asking, "What happened before you _____?" They may or may not be ready to talk. If they are ready, listen intently and repeat back a summary of what you heard to make sure you are both on the same page. Ask what else they could have done instead of the problem behavior. Offer suggestions if they can't come up with any. Take this opportunity to once again help them understand why their behavior was unsafe. Ask if they are ready to return to their friends. This approach may seem to reward children for bad behavior. But it is important to understand that children sometimes need a break from the action to calm down and regain control. Many children do not have cool-down strategies, so leaving them in the same space tends to escalate the situation, while removing them de-escalates it.

If staffing does not allow you to take a child on a walk, consider going to a quiet area of your room and sitting with the child, reading a book or quietly talking about the situation. One program had two posters in its quiet area. One poster showed pictures of problematic things children do, such as pushing, throwing blocks, cutting in line, calling names, knocking down someone's blocks, and tearing someone's artwork. The other poster showed pictures of positive ways to handle similar situations. These posters offered a way for adults to begin conversations with children about problem behaviors and for children to learn other strategies to deal with frustrations. The staff posted other situations as they occurred and other ideas for positive solutions as children generated them.

ASSOCIATED SKILLS

Responsibility

All people face choices every day. Responsibility is being accountable for one's own choices—even the inappropriate ones. Inappropriate choices that young children make can range from name-calling to pushing to stealing to lying. For older children, inappropriate choices may be cheating on tests or not completing assigned chores or homework. Children often want to blame others for their choices because they fear disapproval and negative consequences. At the time of decision, children often believe that they made the right choice. Only when adults react with shock, frustration, sadness, or anger do children realize they might have made an inappropriate choice. It is normal for adults to feel angry or frustrated when children make inappropriate choices. But maintaining an approachable and calm demeanor will help children feel safe even when they realize they have made a mistake. Children can learn from their mistakes only when they feel safe enough to talk about them.

Helping children own their decisions—good and bad—is a gift for life. Taking responsibility for the choices they make is key to getting along with others. Teaching children responsibility begins with helping children understand that everyone makes mistakes, even adults. You can teach children that they cannot do anything to change a mistake that has already happened, but that the most important thing is what they do after the mistake. You can also teach children that when they make mistakes, it is important to be truthful. When people are honest about their mistakes, they can learn from them. Every mistake is a potential learning moment. Teach children how to right their wrongs. You cannot begin to work through a problem with children until all involved parties are calm. Here are some ideas to help children calm down:

- Have the child take a few deep breaths.
- Take a five-minute break.
- Take a walk.
- Listen to music.
- Read a book.
- Color.
- Build with blocks.
- Go to a quiet place.
- Exercise.

After the parties have calmed down, bring them together. Letting all parties tell what happened and why they made the decisions they made is important. Telling their story helps children, adults, and others understand their point of view of the events, how they were feeling, and why they acted as they did. To help children tell their story, ask questions like the following:

- What happened?
- What happened next?
- How did that make you feel?
- What did you do next?

Helping children hear how their decisions made others feel and labeling the emotions will help children understand how their choices affect others. Guide the process from beginning to end, allowing each child to talk about the problem as they see it and come up with solutions. Brainstorm what they could have done differently to produce a different outcome. This brainstorming shows children other options for solving their problems. Once the children agree on a solution, let them try it rather than imposing what you think is a better or fairer solution.

Teaching problem solving is an ongoing process. Often you'll need to modify solutions that do not work. Instill the attitude that "if at first you don't succeed, try, try, try again" (Hickson 1840).

To children, using evasive tactics such as stretching the truth or blaming someone else for the choice that they made seems to work. These tactics may seem pointless and frustrating to you, but they seem like viable options to children. Once you understand the underlying reasons children do not take responsibility for their actions, you can plan activities that teach effective problem solving.

Self-Discipline

Developing self-discipline in youth is the key to becoming responsible adults. Self-discipline is the ability to do what should be done, even when you do not want to. Even if children are well behaved, that does not mean that they would automatically do the right thing. Children who have self-discipline make good choices by weighing the pros and cons of making one choice over another. They take responsibility for the choices they have made. For children to make appropriate choices, they need to take part in setting the rules so they understand why the rules exist.

Teaching children self-discipline at a young age is important. It takes plenty of time and many good role models for children to hone this ability and remember to use it when challenged to do the right thing. Help children learn to wait for others to stop talking rather than interrupting. Provide children with schedules and routines that create a framework for daily living and daily responsibility. Help children learn time management—how to divide their time to accomplish what needs to be done, such as taking a bath, hanging up their coats, putting toys away, doing homework, completing community jobs, and doing fun activities. Give positive feedback when children exhibit self-discipline by describing how they did the right thing. For example, you might say, "That was awesome when you used your words to work out things with Jake," or "Great job choosing to clean up the dramatic play area before I had to remind you." Positive affirmations of a job well done encourage a repeat performance.

Choosing the right response in the middle of conflict, strong emotions, or temptation can be difficult for children. Children's feelings lie close to the surface, and their impulse control is not fully developed. As a result, children will make mistakes and say things that inflame a situation rather than defuse it. Children typically respond to conflict in at least one of these five ways:

- **Seeking:** The child seeks help from an adult to mediate the conflict.
- **Retreating:** The child lets other children have their way and retreats to another activity.
- **Ignoring:** The child ignores the situation and continues to play.
- **Negotiating:** The child resolves the conflict by compromising, and neither child is pleased with the resolution.
- **Collaborating:** The children use empathy to understand each other's point of view and come up with a win-win solution.

Most children will rely on only one or two of these five strategies. Choosing the appropriate strategy is difficult for children. For children to choose, they need to understand all the strategies available to them, so adults need to discuss the pros and cons of each strategy. Role-play each strategy, then engage the children in discussing how they felt and how others would be affected by each solution. This will help children learn different ways to solve conflict and will show them the benefits and challenges of each approach so they can choose the one that best addresses a specific conflict. Help children understand that they need more strategies than simply calling on an adult to solve their problems. Outsourcing problem solving to another person does not help children develop nonviolent conflict resolution skills or responsibility for their words and actions.

Internalizing Self-Control

Internalizing self-control is making responsibility and self-discipline a way of life. Learning responsibility and self-discipline is the first step; it is only when these become a constant part of a child's attitude and way of life that the child has internalized self-control. Here's another way of looking at it: responsibility and self-discipline are the tools you use to control yourself, and internalizing self-control is making use of these tools automatically.

Internalization does not happen overnight. In fact, many adults still have not internalized self-control. When children see adults consistently and fairly creating and enforcing community rules, children learn how control works—and benefits them—in daily life. However, when children see adults behaving inconsistently, children learn that it is OK not to be responsible and self-disciplined all the time. Because internalizing self-control takes time and children will make mistakes, adults need to supply the children with support and a caring, safe environment where children can learn from their mistakes. Have age-appropriate expectations for children. (For example, while toddlers may have learned to self-soothe in distress, they cannot understand the pluses and minuses of various conflict resolution strategies.) With intentional teaching, consistency, patience, and adult support, children can internalize self-control.

PROVIDERS' ROLE

Intentional Teaching

Control is a skill set everyone needs to develop. It involves more than just stopping negative behaviors. It also means choosing appropriate behaviors.

There are many ways in which caregivers of young children can intentionally help them develop control. Move about the room throughout the day and keep tabs on all the children. You will have days when this seems impossible, with disruption everywhere, but preplanning can help you maximize children's self-control. Provide enough materials to meet the needs of however many children are in the classroom. Meanwhile, take care not to overwhelm the children with too many materials, causing them to be so excited that they can't focus on one activity. Provide an environment where children feel safe. Make sure children know that if they make mistakes, you will listen without judgment and help them learn from their mistakes and do better next time. Encourage children to be truthful by being patient and remaining calm. Work with children who have control issues to identify how they feel when they become angry. Teach strategies to help children retain control before acting. Create mantras such as "I can do this" to inspire children to believe in their ability to do the right thing.

Environment Design

Environmental Elements That Foster Control

PHYSICAL ENVIRONMENT	TEMPORAL ENVIRONMENT	INTERPERSONAL ENVIRONMENT
• Reducing number of choices to prevent overstimulation	• Following daily routines	• Giving permission to be alone or separated from group activities
• A quiet space to calm down	• Including children in making rules	• Encouraging children to take control of their own behavior
• Audiobooks and music areas equipped with headphones for individual listening	• Posting rules for each area within the space	• Providing one-on-one time with staff to share emotions
• Stress balls, playdough, fidgets, and slime for stress relief	• Posting self-affirmations within the space, such as I Can Do This, Be Calm, Breathe, Be Kind, and Listen First, with picture cues for nonreaders	• Helping children take responsibility for their actions, such as putting toys away and cleaning up after snack
• Water table with sensory materials, such as sand, water, or dirt	• Warning children three to five minutes before transitioning to a new activity	• Role-playing situations that help children understand others' feelings
	• Minimizing waiting	

Strategies for Intentional Teaching and Encouraging Skill Development

- Help children choose appropriate responses when dealing with conflict or frustration.
- When you are directing children, tell them what you *do* want them to do, not just what you *don't* want them to do.
- Teach de-stressing strategies.
- Help children use breathing techniques to calm themselves.
- Practice control strategies when children are calm and not in conflict.
- Role-play problem-solving scenarios.
- Help children learn the pros and cons of a decision.

PARENT AND STAFF EDUCATION STRATEGIES

Training staff on how to help children gain control is vital. Look to community agencies that may be able to provide these trainings. Assess the environments to make sure they are equipped with areas that support children as they begin to learn the skills associated with control. Formulate discipline policies that provide opportunities for children to learn from their mistakes. Staff need to help create these policies and have a clear understanding of what these policies mean. Intentionally integrate stress-relieving activities into the daily schedule. Staff and parents must recognize that control is often difficult for children, and it takes time to learn each of the associated skills. Use your program's newsletter and website to give families tips to help children internalize self-control, and share what is being done in the program to help the children master this skill. Encourage two-way communications to share when children are under stress or dealing with a difficult situation. Routinely plan face-to-face meetings and conferences to exchange information. Create an open-door policy to encourage parents to regularly and informally share information that might affect children's behavior.

Things to Remember

- Maintaining control consistently is very difficult for children and adults alike.
- Children need to be taught control skills.
- Adults need to plan time intentionally for children to practice control skills.
- More materials and supplies are not necessarily better.
- Children who can manage their behavior can minimize negative behaviors.
- Children respond negatively to inconsistency.
- Children learn how to manage challenges from observing those around them.
- Take time to listen without interrupting when children want to talk.
- Eliminate power struggles whenever possible.
- Children forget rules and expectations, so remind them often.
- Break down instructions into parts to increase compliance.
- Mistakes will happen.

- Outsourcing problem solving to an adult does not help children learn to solve their own problems.
- Internalizing self-control does not happen overnight.

Children's Books Dealing with Control

- *The Angry Dragon* by Michael Gordon
- *Beezus and Ramona* by Beverly Cleary
- *The Golden Key* by Sigal Adler
- *Hands Are Not for Hitting* by Martine Agassi
- *It's Hard to Be Five* by Jamie Lee Curtis and Laura Cornell
- *Raccoons, Revenge, and Strawberry Pie* by Gregory M. Reynolds
- *The Sign of the Beaver* by Elizabeth George Speare
- *Sometimes I'm Bombaloo* by Rachel Vail
- *The Way I Feel* by Janan Cain
- *When I Feel Angry* by Cornelia Maude Spelman

CHAPTER 9

Tying It All Together

Humans are innately social. They need one another. However, people do not always have the social skills needed to interact with others in acceptable ways.

Social skills are the tools humans use to communicate to others how they feel and what they need or want. Social competency consists of seven skill sets that enable people to interact with others successfully: communication, coping, community building, conflict resolution, confidence, curiosity, and control. Social skills overlap and work in concert with one another to help humans navigate many environments and people every day.

Children are not born with social skills, so adults need to teach children these skills intentionally. Children need support and practice to learn and improve these skills. Support comes in the form of a safe, nurturing, and accepting environment. In a safe environment, children are accepted for who they are and can fail without judgment. When social skills are intentionally taught, practiced, and honed, over time children will learn to make appropriate choices while being respectful of others. When children have made an inappropriate choice, they need time to redirect their behavior toward a more acceptable choice. When children fail, adults must provide activities that give children the tools they need to make another choice.

SOCIAL SKILLS ASSESSMENT

Before you begin teaching children social skills, assess where children are, outlining the skills they have and those they lack. Once you know this information, you can plan activities that help children develop missing skills. You can conduct either an informal assessment or a formal assessment (or both). An informal assessment is an observation and a clearly written documentation of the events observed. A formal assessment is a standardized test that systematically measures how well a child has mastered a specific skill or learning outcome.

When you are choosing a formal assessment tool for social competency, consider certain factors. First, determine what you want from the formal assessment. Identify one or more assessment tools that suit your goals and match the ages of the children you serve. Determine what type of training each tool will require to provide reliable results. What will be the total cost for the tool and the training? Decide how you will use the information gained from the assessment. Then choose the assessment tool that best meets your needs. The following list of formal assessment tools can help you get started with your search. This is just a sample of available tests and is not meant to be a comprehensive list.

- The **Social-Emotional Assessment/Evaluation Measure (SEAM)** is a "functional tool for assessing and monitoring social-emotional and behavioral development in infants, toddlers, and preschoolers at risk for social-emotional delays or problems." See www.brookespublishing .com/product/seam.

- The **Ages & Stages Questionnaires: Social-Emotional, Second Edition (ASQ:SE-2)** is a "highly reliable, parent-completed tool with a deep, exclusive focus on children's social and emotional development." You can quickly "pinpoint behaviors of concern, and identify any need for further assessment or ongoing monitoring." See www .brookespublishing.com/product/asqse-2.

- The **Social Emotional Assets and Resilience Scales (SEARS)** focuses on a child's strengths. It can be used with "children and adolescents who exhibit a variety of clinical problems or who are at high risk for developing such problems." It includes "separate assessment forms for children (ages eight to twelve years or grades three to six) and for adolescents (ages thirteen to eighteen years or grades seven to twelve), as well as teacher report forms and parent report forms. The forms may be used for any combination of student, parent, and teacher assessment." See www.parinc.com/Products/PKey/406.

- The **Social Skills Improvement System (SSIS) Rating Scales** enable "targeted assessment of individuals and small groups to help evaluate social skills, problem behaviors, and academic competence. Teacher, parent, and student forms help provide a comprehensive picture across school, home, and community settings."

The SSIS Rating Scales help "measure social skills (communication, cooperation, assertion, responsibility, empathy, engagement, self-control), competing problem behaviors (externalizing, bullying, hyperactivity/inattention, internalizing, autism spectrum), and academic competence (reading achievement, math achievement, motivation to learn)." See www.pearsonclinical.com/education /products/100000322/social-skills-improvement-system-ssis-rating -scales.html.

- The **Behavior Assessment System for Children, Second Edition (BASC-2)** is a "comprehensive set of rating scales and forms including the Teacher Rating Scales (TRS), Parent Rating Scales (PRS), Self-Report of Personality (SRP), Student Observation System (SOS), and Structured Developmental History (SDH). Together, they help you understand the behaviors and emotions of children and adolescents." See www.pearsonclinical.com/education/products /100000658/behavior-assessment-system-for-children-second -edition-basc-2.html.

- The **Devereux Early Childhood Assessment for Preschoolers Second Edition (DECA-P2)**, is a "strength-based assessment and planning system designed to promote resilience in children ages three through five. The kit includes a nationally standardized, strength-based assessment along with strategy guides for early childhood educators and families." See https://centerforresilientchildren.org /preschool/assessments-resources/the-devereux-early-childhood -assessment-preschool-program-second-edition.

- The **Greenspan Social-Emotional Growth Chart** helps you monitor the milestones of social-emotional development in infants and very young children, birth to age three. See www.pearsonclinical.com /childhood/products/100000214/greenspan-social-emotional -growth-chart.html.

- The **Preschool and Kindergarten Behavior Scales Second Edition (PKBS-2)** is a "behavior rating scale designed for use with children ages three through six years. This unique behavior rating scale is easy to use, very practical, and based on a solid foundation of research. With seventy-six items on two separate scales, it provides an integrated and functional appraisal of the social skills and problem behaviors of young children. The scales can be completed by a variety of behavioral informants, such as parents, teachers, and other caregivers." See www.mindresources.com /occupational-therapy/025243.

CREATING AN ACTION PLAN

After you conduct a formal or informal assessment (or both) to determine what social skills children have and lack, you will need to develop an action plan. Your plan should outline how you wish to make changes and create supports and activities to intentionally teach missing skills and hone existing skills. The action plan needs to include a goal, strategies, and outcomes. It should indicate who will be responsible for completing the tasks, the time frame for completion of tasks, and any associated costs. It can also outline the work needed to create an environment (physical, temporal, and interpersonal) better suited to developing social competency. (For a blank action plan form, see appendix E.)

Things to Remember

- Teaching children social skills provides them with tools that they can use for the rest of their lives.
- Positive social skills allow children to get their needs met in socially acceptable ways.
- These skills can be used to develop friendships and interact with others as children in school and later as adults in their professional lives.
- All social skills are interwoven and work together to help children develop social competency.
- Teaching social skills takes time.
- Children forget.
- Role-playing and practicing are important tools for honing social skills with children.
- The physical environment is the center of the community; design yours with spaces that allow children to talk and build relationships with peers.
- Teach relaxation and de-stressing strategies.

- Adults need to identify their own communication style and hot buttons.
- Children need to develop the skill of moving to executive function so they are able to generate appropriate solutions for the problem at hand.
- Curiosity spawns creativity.

APPENDIX A

Observation

Date: _____

Filled out by: _____

Where did the observation happen? Indoors or outdoors? _____

In what area of the indoor or outdoor space did the observation occur?_____

_____

Who was involved? _____

What time of day was it? _____

What happened to cause the conflict? Describe the event using children's names, and quote their conversations. _____

_____

Do these children usually play well together? _____

Were the children taking turns talking to one another, or were they talking over one another during the conflict? Explain, using quotes. _____

_____

Was there pushing, shoving, or hitting? _____

Did a child get hurt? Was an incident report filed? _____

Was there name-calling? _____

Were the children taking turns explaining what happened when discussing the problem with an adult?

_____

Did the environment have enough supplies and materials for all the children to play successfully?

_____

Was a separate place available where the children could go to problem solve and discuss this situation?

_____

Who solved the problem, the children or the adult? _____

Were the children involved able to rejoin play successfully? _____

_____

Next Steps

What were the skill assets? _____

_____

What were the skill deficits? _____

_____

Ideas for intentional teaching activities: _____

_____

Ideas for environmental changes: _____

_____

APPENDIX B

Peace Table Prompts

Invitation

Child 1 Child 2 Tell your story Listen

Child 1 Child 2 Tell your story Listen

List solutions Choose a solution Declare peace together Return to play

APPENDIX C

Writing Prompts

What would you do if . . .

. . . someone ripped your picture?

. . . someone knocked down your building?

. . . someone took your toy?

. . . someone shoved you down?

. . . you spilled your milk?

. . . someone called you a name?

. . . someone yelled at you?

. . . someone hit you?

. . . your ice-cream cone fell on the floor?

APPENDIX D

Sample Pizza-Theme Box Inventory Sheet

☐ 3 cardboard rounds

☐ 4 small plastic plates

☐ 1 Big Deal Pizza Shop sign

☐ 1 container of grated cheese (2-inch lengths of white yarn)

☐ 1 container of green pepper slices (C-shaped green felt)

☐ 1 container of pepperoni (small red felt circles 1.5 inches in diameter)

☐ 3 pads of paper

☐ 3 pencils

☐ 1 Pizza Sold Here sign

☐ 1 red-and-white check tablecloth

☐ 3 crusts (white flexible canvas circles)

☐ 3 tomato sauce pieces (red felt circles as large as the canvas crusts)

☐ 2 aprons

☐ 2 menus

☐ 2 phones

☐ 2 pictures of pizza

☐ Various denominations of play money

Last date used in the program: _____

Replenished on: _____

Replenished by: _____

APPENDIX E

Action Plan

Name of Program: _____

Class: _____

GOAL	STRATEGIES	WHO WILL DO IT	RESOURCES NEEDED	TIMETABLE	DATE COMPLETED
Communication					
Coping					
Community Building					
Conflict Resolution					
Confidence					
Curiosity					
Control					

Completed by: _____ Date: _____

References

AAP (American Academy of Pediatrics). 2016. "American Academy of Pediatrics Announces New Recommendations for Children's Media Use." October 21. www .aap.org/en-us/about-the-aap/aap-press-room/Pages/American-Academy-of -Pediatrics-Announces-New-Recommendations-for-Childrens-Media-Use.aspx.

APA (American Psychological Association). 2012. "Delaying Gratification." www.apa .org/helpcenter/willpower-gratification.pdf.

———. 2018. "Cohort Effects in Children's Delay of Gratification." June 25. www.apa .org/pubs/journals/releases/dev-dev0000533.pdf.

Armstrong, Linda J., and Christine A. Schmidt. 2013. *Great Afterschool Programs and Spaces That Wow!* St. Paul, MN: Redleaf Press.

Ashdown, Daniela Maree, and Michael E. Bernard. 2012. "Can Explicit Instruction in Social and Emotional Learning Skills Benefit the Social-Emotional Development, Well-Being, and Academic Achievement of Young Children?" *Early Childhood Education Journal* 39, no. 6 (January): 397–405.

Baicker-McKee, Carol. 2009. *The Preschooler Problem Solver: Tackling Tough and Tricky Transitions with Your Two- to Five-Year-Old*. Atlanta: Peachtree.

Bailey, Becky A. 1996. *I Love You Rituals*. Oviedo, FL: Loving Guidance.

———. 2015. *Conscious Discipline: Building Resilient Classrooms*. Oviedo, FL: Loving Guidance.

Beaty, Janice J. 1992. *Skills for Preschool Teachers*, 4th ed. New York: Merrill.

Carlsson-Paige, Nancy. 2008. *Taking Back Childhood: Helping Your Kids Thrive in a Fast-Paced, Media-Saturated, Violence-Filled World*. New York: Hudson Street Press.

Center on the Developing Child at Harvard University. 2017. "Three Principles to Improve Outcomes for Children and Families." https://developingchild.harvard.edu /resources/three-early-childhood-development-principles-improve-child-family -outcomes/.

Cleveland Clinic. 2016. "Fostering a Positive Self Image." https://my.clevelandclinic.org /health/articles/12942-fostering-a-positive-self-image.

COCM (Council on Communications and Media). 2009. "Media Violence." *Pediatrics* 124 (5). http://pediatrics.aappublications.org/content/124/5/1495.

Common Sense Media. 2013. "Zero to Eight: Children's Media Use in America 2013." www.commonsensemedia.org/research/zero-to-eight-childrens-media-use-in -america-2013.

Copple, Carol, and Sue Bredekamp. 2009. *Developmentally Appropriate Practice in Early Childhood Programs Serving Children from Birth through Age 8*. Washington, DC: National Association for the Education of Young Children.

Crowe, Caltha. 2009. "Coaching Children in Handling Everyday Conflicts." Responsive Classroom. February 1. www.responsiveclassroom.org/coaching-children-in-handling -everyday-conflicts/.

CSEFEL (Center on the Social and Emotional Foundations for Early Learning). 2018. "Promoting Positive Peer Social Interactions." Accessed August 8. http://csefel .vanderbilt.edu/briefs/wwb8.pdf.

Curtis, Deb, and Margie Carter. 2015. *Designs for Living and Learning: Transforming Early Childhood Environments*. 2nd ed. St. Paul, MN: Redleaf Press.

Division of Sleep Medicine (DSM) at Harvard Medical School. 2008. "Sleep and Mood." December 15, 2008. http://healthysleep.med.harvard.edu/need-sleep/whats-in-it-for -you/mood.

Drew, Walter F. 2007. "Endless Possibilities." *Scholastic Parent and Child*. April. www .isaeplay.org/Resource_Articles/Endless_Possibilities.pdf.

Driver, Janine. 2011. "Baby Body Language." *Psychology Today*. June 3. www.psychologytoday .com/us/blog/you-say-more-you-think/201106/baby-body-language.

Duckworth, Angela L. 2011. "The Significance of Self-Control." *Proceedings of the National Academy of Sciences (PNAS)* 108, no. 7 (February): 2639–40. www.pnas.org /content/108/7/2639.

Dweck, Carol S. 2008a. "Brainology: Transforming Students' Motivation to Learn." National Association of Independent Schools. www.stns.org/downloads/NAISBrainology .CarolDweck.pdf.

———. 2008b. *Mindset: The New Psychology of Success*. Random House Digital.

Elias, Maurice J., and Harriett Arnold, eds. 2006. *The Educator's Guide to Emotional Intelligence and Academic Achievement: Social-Emotional Learning in the Classroom*. Thousand Oaks, CA: Corwin Press.

Encyclopedia of Children's Health. 2017. "Social Competence." Accessed June 8. www .healthofchildren.com/S/Social-Competence.html.

Epstein, Ann S. 2009a. *Me, You, Us: Social-Emotional Learning in Preschool*. Ypsilanti, MI: HighScope Press.

———. 2009b. "Think before You (Inter)Act: What It Means to Be an Intentional Teacher." *Exchange* 185 (January/February): 46–49. https://dcf.wisconsin.gov/files/ccic/pdf /articles/think-before-you-interact.pdf.

Fox, Lise, and Rochelle Harper Lentini. 2006. "'You Got It!' Teaching Social and Emotional Skills." *Young Children* 61, no. 6 (November): 36–42.

Frankel, Fred. 1996. *Good Friends Are Hard to Find: Help Your Child Find, Make, and Keep Friends*. Los Angeles: Perspective.

Frost, Joe L., Pei-San Brown, John A. Sutterby, and Candra D. Thornton. 2004. *The Developmental Benefits of Playgrounds*. Olney, MD: Association for Childhood Education International.

Gordon, Ann Miles, and Kathryn Williams Browne. 2011. *Beginnings and Beyond: Foundations in Early Childhood Education*. 8th ed. Belmont, CA: Wadsworth.

Greenman, James. 2005. *Caring Spaces, Learning Places: Children's Environments That Work*. Redmond, WA: Exchange Press.

Gurian, Anita, and Alice Pope. 2009. "Do Kids Need Friends?" About Our Kids. www .lbusd.org/uploaded/4-EMS/About/Documents/Do_Kids_Need_Friends.pdf.

Hamilton, Jon. 2014. "Scientists Say Child's Play Helps Build a Better Brain." *Morning Edition*. Washington, DC: NPR. Broadcast August 6. www.npr.org/sections/ed/2014 /08/06/336361277/scientists-say-childs-play-helps-build-a-better-brain.

Hamlin, Maria, and Debora B. Wisneski. 2012. "Supporting the Scientific Thinking and Inquiry of Toddlers and Preschoolers through Play." *Young Children* 67, no. 3 (May): 82–88.

Han, Heejeong Sophia, and Kristen Mary Kemple. 2006. "Components of Social Competence and Strategies of Support: Considering What to Teach and How." *Early Childhood Education Journal* 34, no. 3 (December): 241–46.

Hartup, Willard W. 1992. "Having Friends, Making Friends, and Keeping Friends: Relationships as Educational Contexts. ERIC Digest." Educational Resources Information Center (ERIC). www.ericdigests.org/1992-3/friends.htm.

Henderson, Nan, and Mike M. Milstein. 2003. *Resiliency in Schools: Making It Happen for Students and Educators*. 2nd ed. Thousand Oaks, CA: Corwin Press.

Henry J. Kaiser Family Foundation (KFF). 2010. "Daily Media Use among Children and Teens Up Dramatically from Five Years Ago." www.kff.org/disparities-policy/press-release/daily-media-use-among-children-and-teens-up-dramatically-from-five-years-ago/.

Hickson, William Edward. 1840. "Perseverance, or Try Again." In *The Singing Master*, 4th ed., 106–7. London: Taylor and Walton. https://ia600607.us.archive.org/4/items/singoohick/singoohick.pdf.

Huitt, William G., and Courtney Dawson. 2011. "Social Development: Why It Is Important and How to Impact It." *Educational Psychology Interactive* (April): 1–27. www.edpsycinteractive.org/papers/socdev.pdf.

Hurley, Katie. 2015. *The Happy Kid Handbook: How to Raise Joyful Children in a Stressful World*. New York: TarcherPerigee.

Isbell, Rebecca T., and Betty Exelby. 2001. *Early Learning Environments That Work*. Beltsville, MD: Gryphon House.

Johnson, David W., and Roger T. Johnson. 1996. "Conflict Resolution and Peer Mediation Programs in Elementary and Secondary Schools: A Review of the Research." *Review of Educational Research* 66 (4): 459–506.

Kamps, Debra M., Melody Tankersley, and Cynthia Ellis. 2000. "Social Skills Interventions for Young At-Risk Students: A 2-Year Follow-Up Study." *Behavioral Disorders* 25, no. 4 (August): 310–24.

Katz, Lilian G., and Diane E. McClellan. 1997. *Fostering Children's Social Competence: The Teacher's Role*. National Association for the Education of Young Children Washington (NAEYC).

Kennedy-Moore, Eileen, and Christine McLaughlin. 2017. *Growing Friendships: A Kids' Guide to Making and Keeping Friends*. New York: Aladdin.

Kohn, Alfie. 2006. *Beyond Discipline: From Compliance to Community*. 2nd ed. Alexandria, VA: Association for Supervision and Curriculum Development (ASCD).

Krapp, Kristine, and Jeffrey Wilson. 2016. *The Gale Encyclopedia of Children's Health: Infancy through Adolescence*. 3rd ed. Farmington Hills, MI: Gale Cengage Learning.

LeBoeuf, Donni, and Robin V. Delany-Shabazz. 1997. "Conflict Resolution. Fact Sheet #55." Department of Justice, Office of Juvenile Justice and Deliquency Prevention. https://files.eric.ed.gov/fulltext/ED416301.pdf.

Lehrer, Jonah. 2009. "Don't! The Secret of Self-Control." *The New Yorker*. May 18, 2009. www.newyorker.com/magazine/2009/05/18/dont-2.

Levine, Madeline. 2012. *Teach Your Children Well: Parenting for Authentic Success*. New York: Harper.

Li, Junlei, and Michael Robb. 2015. "Open-Ended versus Single-Action Play in the Digital World." Fred Rogers Center (blog). June 16. www.fredrogerscenter.org/2015/06/open-ended-versus-single-action-play-in-the-digital-world/.

Lynch, Sharon A., and Cynthia G. Simpson. 2010. "Social Skills: Laying the Foundation for Success." *Dimensions of Early Childhood* 38 (2): 3–12.

Mercer, Sarah, and Stephen Ryan. 2010. "A Mindset for EFL: Learners' Beliefs about the Role of Natural Talent." *ELT Journal* 64 (4): 436–44.

Miller, Lisa. 2015. *The Spiritual Child: The New Science on Parenting for Health and Lifelong Thriving*. New York: St. Martin's Press.

Miller, Susan A. 2017. *Social Development of Three- and Four-Year-Olds*. Lewisville, NC: Gryphon House.

Moffitt, Terrie E., Louise Arseneault, Daniel Belsky, Nigel Dickson, Robert J. Hancox, HonaLee Harrington, Renate Houts, et al. 2011. "A Gradient of Childhood Self-Control Predicts Health, Wealth, and Public Safety." *Proceedings of the National Academy of Sciences of the United States of America (PNAS)* 108, no. 7 (February): 2693–98. doi.org/10.1073/pnas.1010076108.

Morris, Pamela, Shira K. Mattera, Nina Castells, Michael Bangser, Karen Bierman, and Cybele Raver. 2014. "Impact Findings from the Head Start CARES Demonstration: National Evaluation of Three Approaches to Improving Preschoolers' Social and Emotional Competence." MDRC. www.mdrc.org/sites/default/files/HSCares_2014%20 Impact%20Report.pdf.

Musson, Steve. 1994. *School-Age Care: Theory and Practice*. Don Mills, ON: Addison-Wesley.

NASP (National Association of School Psychologists). 2002. "Social Skills: Promoting Positive Behavior, Academic Success, and School Safety." www.naspcenter.org /factsheets/socialskills_fs.html.

———. 2015. "How Children Cope with Ongoing Threat and Trauma: The BASIC Ph Model." www.nasponline.org/resources-and-publications/resources/school-safety -and-crisis/trauma/how-children-cope-with-ongoing-threat-and-trauma.

Ollhoff, Jim, and Laurie Ollhoff. 2007. *Getting Along: Teaching Social Skills to Children and Youth*. Farmington, MN: Sparrow Media Group.

Pawlina, Shelby, and Christie Stanford. 2011. "Preschoolers Grow Their Brains: Shifting Mindsets for Greater Resiliency and Better Problem Solving." *Young Children* 66, no. 5 (September): 30–35.

Peterson, Ralph. 1992. *Life in a Crowded Place: Making a Learning Community*. Portsmouth, NH: Heinemann.

Piaget, Jean. (1951) 2013. *Play, Dreams and Imitation in Childhood*. New York: Routledge.

Pinker, Susan. 2015. *The Village Effect: How Face-to-Face Contact Can Make Us Healthier and Happier*. Toronto: Vintage Canada.

Plowman, Lydia, and Joanna McPake. 2013. "Seven Myths about Young Children and Technology." *Childhood Education* 89 (1): 27–33.

Rath, Tom, and Donald Clifton. 2004. *How Full Is Your Bucket?* New York: Gallup Press.

Reid Chassiakos, Yolanda, and Corinn Cross. 2017. "Young Minds and Media." Slideshow presentation.

Rogers McEvoy, Victoria. 2012. *Taming Your Child's Temper Tantrums*. New York: RosettaBooks.

Ross, Ruth Herron, and Beth Roberts-Pacchione. 2011. *Making Friends PreK–3: A Social Skills Program for Inclusive Settings*. Thousand Oaks, CA: Corwin Press.

Schiller, Pam. 2009. "Program Practices That Support Intentionality in Teaching." *Exchange* 185 (January): 57.

Schwartz, Katrina. 2013. "How Free Play Can Define Kids' Success." MindShift. February 15, 2013. www.kqed.org/mindshift/27124/how-free-play-can-define-kids-success.

Shanker, Stuart. 2016. *Psychology Today*. "Self-Regulation vs. Self-Control." www .psychologytoday.com/usblog/self-reg-self-regulation-vs-self-control.

Sigman, Aric. 2012. "The Impact of Screen Media on Children: A Eurovision for Parliament." *Improving the Quality of Childhood in Europe* 3:88–121. www.steinereducation .edu.au/wp-content/uploads/uk_screen_time.pdf.

Spence, Susan H., Caroline Donovan, and Margaret Brechman-Toussaint. 2000. "The Treatment of Childhood Social Phobia: The Effectiveness of a Social Skills Training–Based, Cognitive-Behavioural Intervention, with and without Parental Involvement." *Journal of Child Psychology and Psychiatry* 41 (6): 713–26.

Squires, Jane, and Diane Bricker. 2007. *An Activity-Based Approach to Developing Young Children's Social Emotional Competence*. Baltimore: Paul H. Brookes.

Standage, Martyn, Sean P. Cumming, and Fiona B. Gillison. 2013. "A Cluster Randomized Controlled Trial of the Be the Best You Can Be Intervention: Effects on the Psychological and Physical Well-Being of School Children." *BMC Public Health* 13:666. doi.org/10.1186/1471-2458-13-666.

Starke, Kathryn. 2012. "Encouraging Creativity in Children." *Education Digest*, 78, no. 4 (December): 57–59.

Taylor, Rebecca D., Eva Oberle, Joseph A. Durlak, and Roger P. Weissberg. 2017. "Promoting Positive Youth Development through School-Based Social and Emotional Learning Interventions: A Meta-Analysis of Follow-Up Effects." *Child Development* 88 (4): 1156–71.

UN Office of the High Commissioner for Human Rights (UN Human Rights). 1990. "Convention on the Rights of the Child." Last updated November 18, 2002. www.ohchr .org/en/professionalinterest/pages/crc.aspx.

Vygotsky, Lev S. 1967. "Play and Its Role in the Mental Development of the Child." *Soviet Psychology* 5 (3): 6–18. doi.org/10.2753/RPO1061-040505036.

———. 1990. "Imagination and Creativity in Childhood." *Soviet Psychology* 28 (1): 84–96. doi.org/10.2753/RPO1061-0405280184.

Waters, Everett, and L. Alan Sroufe. 1983. "Social Competence as a Developmental Construct." *Developmental Review* 3 (1): 79–97.

Webster-Stratton, Carolyn, Jamila Reid, and Mary Hammond. 2001. "Social Skills and Problem-Solving Training for Children with Early-Onset Conduct Problems: Who Benefits?" *Journal of Child Psychology and Psychiatry* 42 (7): 943–52.

Zero to Three. 2004. "The Power of Play." www.zerotothree.org/resources/311-the-power -of-play.

Index

from preschoolers' perspective, 88–89
relationships and, 87
from schoolagers' perspective, 89–91
nonsuccess, helping children deal with, 45–46
nonverbal communication skills, 11, 26–27, 34–35

Ollhoff, Jim, 2
Ollhoff, Laurie, 2
open-ended materials, 111–112
open-ended questions
adults', to clarify, 51
children's "why" questions, 120
examples of adults', 14

Panksepp, Jaak, 15
parents
helping children verbalize emotions, 31–33
improving own communication skills, 40
review of digital platforms by, 29
teaching listening skills, 26
teaching nonverbal communication skills, 27
using verbal communication with young children, 25–26
working with child care providers
creative process and, 124
to develop social skills, 19
information about stressors, 43, 54
See also adults
passive-aggressive communication, 36
passive communication, 36
Pawlina, Shelby, 99
peaceable community
journaling prompts, 93, 149
peace table methodology, 91–93, 147
philosophy, 91
peer teaching
environment to support, 46
positive self-image and, 104
projects that support, 72

Pellis, Sergio, 15
personal space, idea of, 80
physical environment
defining, 9
elements to foster
communication, 38–39
community building, 76
confidence, 108
conflict resolution, 95
control, 136
coping, 56
curiosity, 123
Piaget, Jean, 15
play
area themes, 115–116
benefits of, 13–16, 18
creating opportunities for open-ended, 14
as creative reworkings to construct new realities, 15
curiosity and, 111
designing environments for, 17, 46
free, 16, 17, 49
influence of media on, 112–113
materials for, 111–112, 115
as United Nations recognized right of children, 13
PNAS, 127
Pope, Alice, 62
positive self-image, 102–104
positive self-talk, 101, 102
praise, 100–101
Preschool and Kindergarten Behavior Scales Second Edition (PKBS-2), 141–142
preschoolers
conversations with, 26
friendships of, 62–63
helping
with fearful temperament participate, 116
understand nonverbal communication, 34–35
negotiation as conflict to, 88–89
occupancy visual aids for, 54–55
vocabulary growth of, 31
ways of expressing emotions, 31–32
privacy, digital communication policies to protect, 40

problem solving. See conflict resolution

reality versus fantasy, 82, 83, 84
relaxation techniques. See calming techniques
responsibility
defining, 131
for emotions and behaviors, 44, 51
fostering, 74–75
learning from mistakes and, 131–132
self-control and, 134–135
role-playing, to develop social skills, 22
rules
consistent application of, 6–8
including children in making, 60–61, 75
navigating different environments with different, 129–130

scavenger hunts, 120–121
schedules
importance of, 119–120
negative behavior and, 127
stress and, 121
schoolagers
example of negotiation among, 89–91
friendship groups, 65–66
helping
with fearful temperament participate, 116
understand nonverbal communication, 34–35
vocabulary of, 33
screen time, 28, 29
self-confidence and messages of incapability, 45
self-control, 52–53, 127, 134–135
See also control
self-discipline, 133–135
self-image, positive, 102–104
self-regulation skills, developing through play, 15
self-soothing, 30, 54
sense of acceptance, 106–107
sense of capability, 104–105
sensory tables, 121

single-purpose materials, 112
small-motor coordination, 14–15, 104–105
social comparisons and identity development, 55
social competency, 2, 5
social competency skills
    acquiring, 5, 11
        role-playing and, 22
        through play, 13–14, 18
    action plan, 142, 153
    assessment of
        tools for, 140–142
        which child has and which child does not have, 10–11, 139
    benefits of teaching positive, 12–13
    communication. *See* communication
    community building. *See* community building
    confidence. *See* confidence
    conflict resolution. *See* conflict resolution
    control. *See* control
    coping. *See* coping
    curiosity. *See* curiosity
    described, 1
    learning process, 10–12
    modeling of, 2
        listening strategies, 37
        nonverbal skills, 27, 35
        self-control and, 135
        self-discipline, 133
        verbal skills, 26
    one-time demonstration versus mastery of, 18
    prefrontal cortex of brain management of, 5
    things to remember, 142–143
Social-Emotional Assessment/ Evaluation Measure (SEAM), 140

Social Emotional Assets and Resilience Scales (SEARS), 140
Social Skills Improvement System (SSIS) Rating Scales, 140–141
Stanford, Christie, 99
Stark, Kathryn, 115
startle reflex, 34
stress
    behaviors and, 43, 127
    children with fearful temperament and, 45–46
    conflicts induced by, 79–80
    environmental causes of, 43–44
    helping children deal with, 44–46, 118–120
    reducing, in children, 49, 54–55, 118–120, 121
success
    celebrating and maximizing, 40, 42
    child's definition of, 102, 104
    mastery and one-time, 18
    truthful praise and, 100

temperament
    for adventure, 116
    behaviors and, 1
    friendship skills development and, 62
    social competency and, 2
    types of, 1–2, 9–10
temporal environment
    defining, 8
    elements to foster
        communication, 38–39
        community building, 76
        confidence, 108
        conflict resolution, 95
        control, 136
        coping, 56
        curiosity, 123
theme boxes, 116, 151
time management, 133
    See also schedules

toddlers
    proximity and friendships of, 62
    sense of capability of, 104
    use of body language by and with, 34
    verbal communication of two-year olds, 25
    ways of expressing emotions, 30–31
    See also preschoolers
total body relaxation, 119

unscheduled time, importance of, 113

verbal communication, 25–26
    vocabulary of preschoolers, 31
    vocabulary of schoolagers, 33
    vocabulary of young schoolagers, 33
violence
    helping children find alternatives to, 84–86, 87
    media and, 82–83
    natural aversion to, 86–87
visual aids, 54–55
visualization, 119
Vygotsky, Lev, 15

working memory, described, 52
written, communication skills, 27

"Young Minds and Media" (Chassiakos and Cross), 28–29
young schoolagers
    access to digital communication, 28
    conversations with, 26
    importance of friends to, in new environment, 63–65
    vocabulary of, 33

Zero to Three, 13–14